Your Creative Business: from craft hobbyist to solopreneur, step-by-step

Publishing Data

First edition published 2021

Text copyright Angie Scarr and Kira Swales

Illustration composites and photographs copyright Frank Fisher and Angie Scarr

Design by Frank Fisher

(Some elements altered from Canva professional templates).

Plaza De Andalucía 1, Campofrío, 21668, Huelva, Spain.

ISBN 9798594863064

*To each other, and to the
mother-daughter creative bond*

Contents

Preface

This collaboration came about because I (Angie), and my daughter (Kira) have always had a shared passion for crafting but have completely different craft businesses. Over the years we have also developed a very real respect for the other's areas of expertise and now constantly draw on each other's knowledge. This book answers the sort of questions I ask Kira and the sort of questions Kira asks me. As well as some which we've been asking each other and have had to go away and research the answers to. The book is laid out in subject sections and sometimes as if we are chatting to each other, or with you, guiding each other through our ideas of the principles of running a successful business. Sometimes the questions are real between us and sometimes they are what I imagine you could be asking. If you find the young smart approach to business more useful, you can skip to that. If, on the other hand, you want to read the easy chatty bits before you get to the core of the matter,

you can do that too. We hope it will be both inspiring and informative. You can choose whether you're having a coffee-and-feet-up day or a business-like day. That's not to say that my pieces don't contain some business sense, nor that Kira's aren't chatty. You'll get the idea. For more information about the authors, please read the author biographies at the back of the book.

Note on the first edition

This edition has been rushed out (at my insistence) to meet the needs of the many people who are struggling to find a direction and some courage in the wake of job losses and extreme changes in work and life in the past year of 2020. There may be errors or omissions, and so changes may need to be made to further editions. We hope you will find the information helps support you in your business choices.

Introduction

So, you've been thinking of starting a craft business and wondering whether you have everything you need to make it a success. Or, you may be like me several years ago, having come to a point where finances are too tight and something must be done to get you on track to make a proper living. That's why we wrote this book: to reassure you that absolutely can be successful, and to show you the nuts and bolts of how. Of course, it's going to take some effort, some new learning and quite a lot of courage. Nothing you haven't done before, right?

This book is co-written by a mother-daughter duo: me, Angie Scarr, drawing on 30 years experience of running a miniatures business, and by Kira Swales, who currently has seven years of copywriting and online marketing experience.

Between us we show you many of the benefits and drawbacks of running your own small craft business part time or full time. Kira's side business is part time, while working in eCommerce copywriting and SEO. Mine has been full time.

We give you some useful tricks to make sure you hit the ground running and continue to enjoy your business as if it were still your hobby. Or treat your hobby business as if it were a "proper" business so that it pays you for your time and effort.

We tell you how to value your time or price your work correctly.

We help you with your artist impostor syndrome.

We show you how to deal with difficult customers.

We encourage you to get your strategy together when you feel overwhelmed.

If anyone has ever said your work is too expensive... or too cheap, If words like algorithm and metadata make your brain go fuzzy, If you are like I was years ago, full of creative ideas but without the business know-how to back it up, this book is going to help and reassure you through the toughest bits.

During my business life I have made all the mistakes. But, with a serious illness behind me and retirement looming, a few years ago I decided to put my knowledge to good use and start again. Properly this time.

I did lots of self-revaluing, lots of reading, lots of work on my social media presence and especially on my products and the way I created and sold them. I built several new, more reliable income streams and found, for the first time, that it really is possible to make a living as an artist. Just as importantly, I realised that you can proof yourself against any potential economic or personal changes that life can throw at you. In fact, that's when I realised that I would consider myself a solopreneur, if it weren't for the fact that my husband now actually runs the business, leaving me more time to create.

A solopreneur is someone who runs the entire business themselves and doesn't have staff. Instead they will subcontract the parts of the business that they don't have time for, or experience in. It can be a very effective way to work. For the creative who doesn't wish to step back from their creativity into a managerial role as their business grows, it is the way to work these days. The label is also pretty useful to explain a serious attitude to our creative business if we don't want to be labelled "just a crafter" or "just a writer" or "just a musician". It takes in the whole gamut of marketing, merchandising, blogging, and other paid platforms we may be involved in.

It takes the complexity out of explanations to say "I'm a creative solopreneur" rather than "I'm a miniaturist, inventor of techniques, tool designer, author, who does videos…." and so on.

This book is a distillation of all those years of getting it wrong and those last few finding ways finally to do it right; and, of course, the new marketing knowledge that was often so generously given to me by my daughter. It's written primarily in my voice; however, Kira has contributed throughout.

I hope that, between us, we'll be giving you some inspiration from the idea stage through to the creation of your beautiful work; and on to a fully branded and marketed product. We'll also outline some of the important financial considerations and long-term planning issues. Kira will be bringing you the bang up to date branding and marketing tricks that really work. We'll help you put your name and your products top of the list when your discerning customers come looking for something special. Ideas that work whatever your art or craft.

Best of all we'll chop it all up into manageable chunks for you to dispel those fears we all have when encountering something new and seemingly scary.

1. Your business idea

First thoughts

Let's assume for a moment that, if you haven't already started your business, you already have a good idea and people have asked you if they can buy it. You think there might be a future in it. Congratulations. You're a creator!

Most hobbyists at some time wonder whether to turn their hobby into a business. They want to know whether it will be profitable and whether they would still enjoy it if it became a full-time job. The most frequent worries are "Is my work good enough?", "Will people want to buy it?" and "Will enough people buy my work to make it pay?". Then quickly moving on to worries about taxation and, quite a long way down the preoccupations list, marketing (even though it should really be pretty close to the top of the list). I assume that you are thinking about the ins and outs or have recently started selling your work. You may be wondering if your business has a future as a full-time business, or if it would be better as a "side hustle". Will you be more comfortable with a small extra monthly income, at least enough to cover expenses, or do you really need to go full-time with your craft business?

Maybe you already have a name thought-out, but not much more. You may be a beginner at crafting, may realise you have a passion and talent and you are frustrated at work or at home caring for family members. People have started to buy or to want to buy your work, and you see a dream of getting out of the rat race, but you're scared and hounded by self-doubt. Perhaps you are, understandably, afraid to leave your job for an uncertain income. Maybe you're about to be made redundant and are contemplating a complete change. Typically, money will be tight in your household, and you may feel that you can only make your craft work as a hobby that pays for itself. On the other hand, you might be further along the line and just want a boost of inspiration or a bit of help with the technical stuff.

Of course, there is a very real chance that you haven't yet settled on a product. Until now, you may have just crafted because you enjoy it but have never settled on a niche. You might have been forced to think about self-employment because of uncertainty at work or a sudden change of personal circumstances. We'll have a look at

finding your niche soon. First let's look at the benefits and drawbacks of turning your craft into a business.

> *Takeaway: You may not have an actual product idea decided yet. That shouldn't stop you thinking of yourself as a creator and starting to dream about, and take some of the steps towards, running your own business.*

"What are the benefits of running my own business?"

Being your own boss, never having to kowtow to managers and supervisors, plus choosing your own hours and days of the week have to be the main reasons to choose to be your own boss. These are very closely followed by the need or desire to spend more time with the children or a family member. There are many other reasons too. If your job turns out to be unsatisfying and you crave a change, for example. Some people are driven to create objects that are aesthetically pleasing, and which give others pleasure. For them, nothing else will give them the feeling of satisfaction that creating their own work and selling it will. Some people find it simply impossible to get to a workplace either because of physical or mental illnesses, or other personal circumstances. My own start in the creative business world was brought on by postnatal depression and I understand that this is not at all uncommon. Overall, working from home, creating good quality products and enjoying their work, is simply more sustainable for many people.

You may prefer a part-time or out of work hours 'side-hustle' business. These give you some security. If you lose your job, you still have the business, or if the business doesn't work you still have your job. This can be a really good first step for most people. For some people their craft simply has to pay for the jam on the bread or even just pay for itself. Done in a really businesslike way, a small craft business can convert into a medium size or a big business depending on your dream.

"...and the drawbacks?"

Of course, there are certainly drawbacks to be considered. Perhaps the most important of these being irregular and unpredictable income. The income, at least initially, can be very low. There is no guaranteed wage and no business security. There are no regular weekends off. There is no holiday pay. There are worrying bills. Breakdowns can arrive unexpectedly, and family commitments can suddenly crop up. You can lose your creative "mojo" temporarily, and this can be a concern. You can, and probably will, suffer from self-doubt even more than you would if a salary reinforced your value.

On the other hand, your creative mind can be used to find ways around these problems. The sooner you mitigate against potential bumpy patches, the more likely these will just be little bumps and won't derail you. There are lots of ideas for this in the "other ideas" and "long tail incomes" sections to help you mitigate these problems. Longer term you'll find you have no automatic pension provision. There is also no medical insurance paid for you, if you live somewhere without national healthcare. You will have to build these considerations in for yourself. In Europe you will have to pay varying amounts of national insurance. In some of these countries or states, the level of payment is just as high whether you only make a pound/euro/dollar, or several a month. In many countries you also have to pay sales tax from the very first penny.

> *Takeaway: The best first step you can take is to invest a little time in simply thinking, even if it seems as if you should throw yourself straight in.*

"What should I do first?" Beginning to set goals

If you find yourself with your head spinning with ideas and fears the best thing to do is take notes. Notes help you to calm yourself. It may be a pros and cons list or a mind map or simply stream of consciousness. Just write what you're thinking.

Another way is to set yourself little tasks. Pick up little games. There are loads of free self-realisation ideas on the internet if you want to go away and play a bit. Why not do this one first. It's easy and fun (with serious intent behind it). You can redo this at any time through your business journey.

Your life balance (game)

Take 100 of any small coin token or object such as buttons, counters or even pieces of pasta.

Draw a load of circles or squares with your life goals on them. We've made a few suggestions, but you can add more or even subtract any that aren't important to you.

If you want, you can do it twice. First do your goals and then do your current position, side by side, and find out where you come up short. Take a photo of your two drawings, so you can refer back to them in the future and see how far you've come. Why not make a version to keep your kids occupied, too?

I don't believe that, in life, you can cheat and simply add more tokens. There are some people who believe that you can, and you can buy their "how to have your cake and eat it too" type books. There are plenty of them out there. Some may motivate you, and some may merely make you feel inadequate.

Categories:

Family time/spare time

Happiness/inner contentment

Health and well-being

Respect and/or fame

Relaxation/freedom from anxiety

Outreach/being inspirational/giving/or creating your legacy

Sustainability

Travel/experience

Wealth

I had a friend, who is just starting out, complete this exercise, and this was her result. I hadn't imagined that she would have tokens just left outside the boxes, but I found this interesting. Could she not decide where to put them? Or was there a sort of negative space where everything is still confusing and up in the air?

Don't beat yourself up if you aren't anywhere near to your goals. The idea is that you can simply take a step each day towards taking a piece from one pile and putting it on another which more nearly matches your desired life balance. You can start to make your 5 year

My Goals

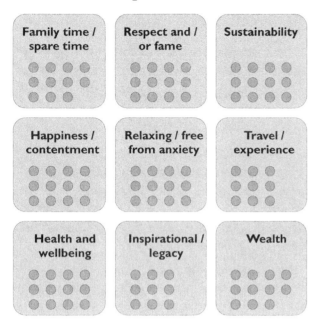

My Current State

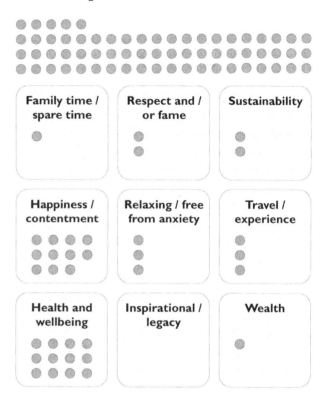

plan with these goals in mind. Some lifestyle coaches call this finding your "why."

It really does help you to know where you are. And the difference between there and where you want to be. Most of us like to think that the health and happiness and family boxes are the ones we really want to fill, but the reality is that sometimes we do need to focus on the money box. For example, one thing crafters often forget is future-proofing (such as building pensions and creating contingency plans), until it's too late. This is covered later. For example, as an older craftsperson who has forgotten about this aspect throughout my life, it hit like a brick when I found myself with ill health in a different country. I had no sickness benefits and my state pension was put back by an extra six years. At that point my "tokens" suddenly had to be shuffled to health and money, with very little time or energy for anything else. So, I had to make a new, more realistic plan.

Takeaway: *The point is it's your dream, your choices, your timetables and your targets you're setting.*

The five year plan

"Why have a five year plan?" Investing in personal development.

Your first decisions about what your business will be, and where you see yourself in your business, start here.

You need to know at a deep level whether you want to 'make it big' or keep it small. Of course, you can change your mind later, but, a little time simply daydreaming can actually be a very wise investment! There are life coaches and the like who make their money out of guiding you to find your inner mission. All you really need to do is ask yourself what you really want and allow yourself to answer without other people's judgments being involved. Just allowing yourself some daydreaming time may save you thousands in personal development courses and therapy in the future. If you then decide that you also need some emotional or professional support, go for it! You don't need to run around for years trying to be an overachiever to justify yourself to others, when all you really want to do is make art and create happiness. On the other hand, if flying around being constantly busy really does float your boat and you really want a boat to float then you simply need to point yourself in a more entrepreneurial direction. Then there's the middle line. An increasing number of people are starting businesses that they want to be successful in but they have no intention of ever having in-house staff with all the payroll accounting and responsibility that entails; instead they become one of an increasing number of new strong solo businesses, now known as solopreneurs. Does that feel like you? I think there's a need to coin another one of those labels. The duopreneur or the co-preneur! That is how I'm beginning to see myself and my husband/business partner.

For the very small business owner, there are several ways of getting something done when you don't know how to do it. One is simply to pay someone else to do it for you, and the other is to invest time and perhaps some money in learning how to do it yourself. There are two more possibilities. You can simply decide to delay it or to ditch it. A good way to contemplate any new task is to choose whether you need to: do it, delegate it, learn it, delay it, or ditch it.

It's always a good idea to keep lists of these jobs and mark next to them which plan you've chosen. Beware "delay" a little, of course, because you end up with loads of half-finished jobs. That, right there, is my major bad habit revealed! But for now, while planning, try putting "do it", "delegate it", "learn it", "delay it" or "ditch it" next to each of the major items you'll have to tackle. That way you'll take the steps to get to your dream of making wonderful things, and getting properly paid for them.

Do it.

Designing, making, marketing and selling. Do you want to do it all yourself? Or is it your dream to have someone else do it for you? Obviously do whatever makes you happy. That's what it's all about. Design and make your first products, but will you want to have some of the repetitive jobs taken off your hands? This book doesn't deal with employment, as that's a whole step away from being a home craft business or even a solopreneur.

It's quite fundamental to the future of your business to find out what you enjoy doing and what you really don't and it's my opinion that if you are spending most of your time doing what you don't enjoy, you need to change your way of working. A five-year plan can help you polarise your plans and not spend a lot of time going down avenues that waste your time and money and sometimes even squash your creativity.

Delegate it.

Deciding whether to pay someone else or to learn a new skill can come down to a time VS money equation. It also depends on whether you enjoy developing new skills and where you want to see yourself on the spectrum between artist and entrepreneur. Only you will know this. Take some time to ask yourself these questions. You can change your mind later, but it does help to have a direction. Do remember to be kind to yourself. The one thing you really can't do is everything.

If you want to make it big, it may be that buying the skills in at a job rate is your most expedient choice. That is to say. You can't be everything at once in a rapidly growing business, so finding the right person to help you may be cheaper in your valuable time than learning to perform certain tasks yourself. This is where you have to also ask yourself whether you want to learn a new skill. If you don't, initially you can look at companies such as Upwork and Fiverr to supply you with people to do small one off jobs outside of your current knowledge. This can work really well for logo design but for ongoing marketing you need to make the decision whether it may be worth investing time in developing your knowledge. Especially if there is some aspect that you really don't enjoy.

Learn it.

Simply being afraid to learn new skills can hold you back too. So you shouldn't avoid being temporarily uncomfortable while learning a new skill that will make you happier and more autonomous in the long term. The upside can be that you remain truly in control. The downside is that you have to try to be all things at the same time.

For the very small business, there may be no option. Fortunately, the most creative people are usually blessed with the most enquiring minds and a joy of learning.

A very real upside of learning to do it yourself is that you can have ideas on the fly and simply realise them in the time it takes to write them down, take a few photos and make a few keystrokes. The downsides are how much time learning it all takes from the process of actually making your product.

Delay it.

There are some things you know you're going to come across but aren't ready to deal with yet. As long as you're honest with yourself about the fact, you'll have to make a decision eventually if you want to be successful.

Delaying some of the tough work or decisions until you are in a stronger place can be a master stroke in the best use of your time.

You need to take a good hard look at where you see yourself in 5 years and decide how much you want to achieve in that time. How much you believe you can achieve. Think through the steps and daydream about being successful. Most importantly your daydreaming may reveal to you whether you'll enjoy it. You don't want to imagine spending the next 5 years not having any fun for an uncertain future. Much better to have fun on the way to where you want to be.

Ditch it

Don't be afraid of ditching a bad idea if, when you look at it, it leaves you feeling cold, or if you experience any feelings of real antipathy. That fork in the road probably isn't for you. You pretty much should feel joy when you think about the future of your business. A little nervousness is normal (see the next section). Dread is not normal or useful. If you find yourself wanting to write "ditch it", go ahead and ditch it. It's very difficult to be successful in something that doesn't make you feel good.

Takeaway: If you are right at the beginning, flip through this book. You don't have to have the mental energy to chew it all up now. Many of the questions you will ask when planning the next 5 years will be answered there. You can jump around as much as you like.

"I'm scared. Today I think it all looks impossible"

It's natural to be anxious about your art, and you will have days when you wonder if your work is any good at all. And you're sure you've over priced it and that everyone will say so. This is commonly referred to as imposter syndrome. Most creatives have massive self-doubt. That can drive you to improve. You shouldn't be afraid of this incredibly common creator problem. In fact the only creatives who never suffer from self-doubt might in fact not question themselves even enough to make anything innovative.

Expect the challenges. Relish them. Take the positives. You're doing something new. Be philosophical about the mistakes. The best things I have ever done in my life came as the result of fairly big mistakes. Sometimes doing things the wrong way throws up a new right way.

When you are contemplating entering the world of business for the first time it can be scary. Just like any change in your life. But don't be daunted. Let me use a little metaphor from my own life to help you take a deep breath and break it down to one small section at a time to look at first.

Nothing worth doing is easy at first. But none of it stays terrifying once you've done it a couple of times.

When I first decided to move to Spain, I found the cities terrifying. It seemed to me symbolic of all the terror involved in any big life decision. The language was fast and unintelligible even though I had A level Spanish. The food was strange and difficult to choose. The traffic was a nightmare. We had to learn not only a new side of the road but new road layouts some of which weren't even on our new satnav (and satnav was also new at the time.) There seemed only to be one way through the city. This involved taking an invisible right turn into a narrow underpass. If we missed one we ended up in the impenetrable city centre only to be shouted at by police, passers-by and our own frazzled partner. It was like my mind had to cope with more new input than it was possible to process.

But, without conquering those fears and obtaining the necessary pieces of paper, we had no hope of getting to our new life. So we did them, one by one. Working out which was the most important piece of paper to acquire first and then leaving the next one until we'd calmed down from the first foray. Step by step. Now we know the city roads, we've done it before and survived. Our life is immeasurably the better for the small courageous steps we took even though at the time they made our heads spin.

So when I realised in my early 60s, I had several whole new areas of learning to undertake to set my business up for the next decade or so I was initially a bit flummoxed but I took a few deep breaths. Blew out and got started. And, of course, I had the help of my daughter along the way, as she was a good few steps ahead of me in some areas.

We have to realise that at any age we can learn new ways of doing things, in exactly the same way as I learned to pick up machine gun speed Spanish in the city streets of Seville and Huelva. The alternative is certainly a lot less exciting, and a lot less profitable.

Most of us feel lost or confused at the beginning of any project or any stage of a new project. Often we just need to know that the help is out there or that something exists. When we do find out it's often a facepalm moment. But we needn't be embarrassed. It happens to us all. For example I've been writing for years but never knew about editing tools. In fact I had never used Google Docs before. To be honest I didn't know either existed until my daughter told me, after a couple of years of frustration about my schoolgirl errors. She didn't know...that I didn't know! Maybe she assumed that I did because I'd already written books. It could be down to mislabelling. If I'd labelled myself a writer all this time I might have talked to more writers and learned more about the technicalities. This made us think about your journey. We might point out things that you already know in this book in order to pick up those people who just don't. Our experience also helped us not to assume that our readers already know.

So what you need to do is to identify the bits of learning that you need which are easiest or the most interesting, or give you the next step on your journey. Take them step-by-step until they are no longer terrifying. You may hear people talk about SMART goals; those are just a way of thinking about taking those steps one by one by setting small targets. It stands for Specific, Measurable, Achievable, and Time-based. There is an important point in both this, and the idea that you can chop big scary tasks into bite sized chunks (often known as "how to eat an elephant").

> *Takeaway*: Everything is easy when you know how to do it. And learning how to do it is just a process, so break it down into manageable steps.

"How will I know if I can solve problems like a "proper businessperson?"

'Every solution has a problem!'

This misquotation is just a little joke at the expense of those people who are stuck in that way of thinking. I know people who are incredibly clever but get stuck too easily at "I can't." The actual quotation which I prefer is more like "every problem has within it the seeds of a solution."

There are many ways you can turn around your thinking from negative to positive in order to achieve what may seem impossible at first. I may be preaching to the converted here, because you picked up this book, so you are clearly looking for your next step. If you apply that same positive turnaround to most of your problems, you'll get to the place you want to be.

> *Anecdote*: I have a little lesson I teach Spanish kids who are learning English. It's a good fun class about getting into the flow of speaking and it comes at the stage when we are flipping from learning simple sentences to thinking in the target language. The lesson consists mainly of a stunt where I walk at the door and bump straight into it and then look dazed and confused. The kids all laugh and then they're on my side. This class serves three purposes. One purpose is to clown my way into opening their minds. The second is to say, "never get stuck on trying to build a thought into a sentence exactly as you think it should be constructed". The closed door symbolises the word they get stuck on if they only have one single way of thinking through the sentence, of course meaning they can go no further. The third purpose is to show by my actions that messing around and not being afraid to make a fool of yourself, can get results.
> I can then explain to them that they can try knocking on the door, but if there's nobody there they are better going around the back and finding an open door, or even climbing in the window. So, in language, the back door is a different construction of the sentence using a different word. The window is throwing the lot out and finding another way to express yourself. They can, using the word "window" as an example, simply say "the glass in a house".
>
> Just as trying to construct the perfect sentence can hinder effective communication, blindly accepting that something can't be done just because it's never been tried or never been tried another way can hinder effective problem solving.

> *Takeaway*: When you see a problem, and that problem doesn't have an obvious solution, that's the closed door at which most people simply walk away. Successful and creative people will first knock on the door, second try to find another door, then finally may climb in the window, metaphorically speaking.

2. Initial considerations

What shall I make? Daydreaming time!

Not everyone has a product idea already. You may be a creative person who has been thrown into the position of having to be self-employed, such as when needing to look after sick relatives or losing your job, for example. If you're still undecided, you'll need some focusing exercises. If you go too far down the wrong path, it can be very expensive and could, ultimately, collapse an embryonic business. Especially if you later find out you actually don't have that much of a passion for your product.

If you don't already have a product in mind, here are a few exercises to help you narrow down your ideas.

Exercise 1: Mind mapping

Sit down and map your creative passions and your abilities. Examples below show a few different ways of doing it. Mine is somewhat crowded because of my age, my full life and my somewhat undisciplined way of working.

Don't allow more than two negatives. If a negative has a positive side, you can remove that negative until you are only left with a maximum of two.

Why do I want you to do this? Because most people spend their whole lives mislabelled. Most of us are forced around the age of 16 to decide who we are and allow ourselves to be labelled and maybe we don't really know then. Maybe we still don't know. Most of us go around with slightly or very much the wrong label stuck to us. It causes us to waste a lot of time going in the wrong direction and knocking on the wrong doors. Even between creative people there are different abilities and it's important that you recognise yours. These exercises can help stop you going down a road that doesn't suit you.

I spent the last 30 years calling myself a miniaturist. But I'm not that! Or at least not specifically and exclusively that. Half the skills needed to be the "best of the best" miniaturist, I lack, or I'm not interested in. I have no ability to design attractive scenes but, given time to think, I can find a way of doing almost everything more quickly, more effectively or more realistically. I finally realised that I have two important sides to what my skills actually are, and they are related. I'm a problem solver, and I'm a teacher. I have a passion for breaking problems down (in three dimensions) to their constituent parts and finding ways of resolving them. In the case of miniatures, I can

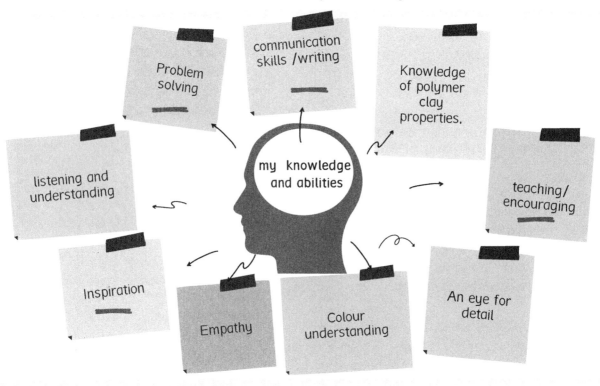

find ways of reproducing what we see in nature. This is because I have a love of colour first and form second. And I have an almost synesthetic love of words for the same reason. I love breaking down communication into similar problems and solutions, and this plays into my teaching and writing skills.

But I spent most of my life not focusing on these skills I had. Instead, I battled with what I didn't have and often what I didn't enjoy, because I thought that was what I ought to do. Rather than following my very real abilities, I was making a hash of the things I did badly. Going in slightly the wrong direction, just because I'd misidentified myself simply as "a miniaturist". Giving myself the correct labels (problem solver, teacher and writer) enabled me to decide on the value and price of my skills. These are of course still largely in the craft field and more specifically in miniatures, but I also like to dabble in writing about politics and philosophy. And now I know I'm not the kind of miniaturist who specialises in "mise en scene". I'm the kind who simply finds ways of doing things no one has thought of before. This is where I'm truly happy. And, unsurprisingly, that is where I can actually earn a living.

I'd like to help you not to waste so many years with the wrong labels like I did. This should help you maximise your positive assets and minimise time spent going down the wrong path. Try filling these labels in with your skills, and not necessarily your job title, to get a real overview of who you really are skills-wise.

Exercise 2: Narrowing down your ideas

Write down up to 10 ideas for broad product groups you might be interested in (examples might include jewellery, illustration or painting, clothing, cosmetics, ceramics, knitting or crochet, calligraphy, glass blowing, metalwork, or artisan food products). If you're stuck, ask yourself what you have made in the past that was the most fun? What have you seen other people doing that was the most fun? Use groups rather than specifics. And then narrow down by removing groups that would cost too much to start, unless they are the ones that most excite you! Now remove any that you have no room for in your home or outhouse, etc. Again, unless they are the ones that most excite you. Excitement gives you the edge in decision making, and that's not always a bad thing.

Take each one of the narrowed down lists onto another page and write as many different products within that group as you can currently think of. When you look at this list, does it fill you with excitement or dread? Do you already know how to do it, or do you have to learn?

When you think about learning, feel for the bubble of excitement or the dread again. Sometimes it can be different to discern between the two. Write down how it makes you feel and sleep on it. Narrow down further the next day. When you're down to two ideas, you can start putting pros and cons on to the lists.

If you really want to do something specific, but feel you lack some of the skills, can you afford to take an intensive course? If, for example, you have a generous redundancy pay, perhaps you could try investing in a course in each of the two final items on your list and then choosing between them. Otherwise, you need to start by going with your gut and figuring out what you can teach yourself. Honestly though, you can change your mind later. After telling you it can be costly to go down the wrong road, I'll remind you that it can be even more costly not to reverse out of a bad choice. Forgive yourself and move on!

Takeaway: Making poor decisions and having the courage to admit you were wrong and change your mind is not a weakness. In fact, flexible thinking and a little humility can make you infinitely powerful. Making decisions doesn't mean you can't change them. It's just a tool to give you direction. Regardless of whether you CAN do something, should you? Will you still be happy doing it in 5 years' time?

Skills you may need to learn

When you find something you would like or need to learn, it's a very good idea to have a notebook or online notebook. You can note down your thoughts and any free or reasonably priced learning solutions that you've seen. Often, the best place to start is with YouTube videos as you can very quickly find out whether someone's teaching style works for you. Then you can buy their training or books if you think they are going to help you get to where you want to be more quickly. Be aware that some of these people may be very good at marketing for example. This may be what you're looking for. But watch out for slick marketing with nothing behind it. These aren't exactly cons, but they can be low-value training products. Most business and marketing software and apps are well covered with training products for free and your greatest cost is in time, watching and experimenting with these free versions. When you find an assistant or course you really can work with, go for it. But be selective. Don't underestimate the value of paying for courses or one-off classes to improve your business, as this can be an investment that pays itself.

Personally, I think of learning as a double investment. Learning in itself gives me a sense of achievement (even at my advanced age). Then I have saved myself paying someone else over and over to keep doing things I can now quickly do myself. So, I am still continuously learning. Some of the skills which we will present in the marketing section are Kira's and are still on my wishlist. Try to limit your engagement time with expensive software and apps, and leave time for considering whether this or another, simpler, solution will be best for you.

There is one skill I will never learn, and it's the one dealt with below. I decided a long time ago that I was not interested in picking up accountancy. This is why I really want to simplify it and debunk the fear for you. Because it was and still is my least favourite aspect of running a business. If you enjoy accountancy and you're good at it, please feel free to skip my simplifications below. Nobody should skip the processes of making business cash flow forecasts (coming up soon) though. Even if you need someone to help you with that.

Don't be afraid of setting a realistic budget for buying in paid help with accountancy and cash flow forecasting if these things worry you. It will take a very unpleasant weight off your shoulders. Hand it to someone who can do it better for less than the price of a coffee a day. I'd give up a coffee to give all my nasty paperwork to someone else. A small business shouldn't expect to pay more than 100 a month for accountancy services. You can get it down to about 300 a year (I can't write which currency, but it shouldn't be much more, even in the lowest exchange rate currency).

Takeaway: Developing real flexibility to dealing with problems will be your greatest strength in business and in life. If you really do see every problem as a challenge, every challenge as a learning opportunity and every learning opportunity as an extra skill you can give back to your business, you will enjoy almost every day of your life. How great is that?

3. Money matters

Funding and cash flow

You need to know that you can live on the money you will bring in before you go full time. So it may be that you will have to be part time, earning at least some reliable income while you invest the rest of your time into the initial set up. Another option is to see if there are any business support grants in your area, as you might be surprised. Ask your local council if they have any new business support schemes. Try the government websites mentioned in the section below on "The dreaded taxman" for information on government business support grants, as well as registration and tax advice.

Starting out selling with good pricing crucial to ensuring your business is sustainable, and we'll delve into that in the next chapter. You'll also find information in the "moving to multiple income streams" (Chapter 16) to help you find more ways to scrape through the first years. These will boost you in the next few, so getting started with those is a real investment.

It may be that you need to have an extremely frugal year in order to get on track. The cost of a couple of books on the subject should be one of your investments. I have a book called *The Frugalist* out under a pseudonym (ISBN: 978-84-122029-0-8), recommended for those who don't mind a bit of politics and ecology in their reading, and who are facing a tight year or three. Other books on living frugally are available, too.

This is not a book on accountancy nor on how to apply for a loan from your bank. However, if you're going to your bank manager or even to a generous family member for financial support, it never hurts to have a basic understanding of your cash flow forecast.

Cash flow forecasts are not the same as accountancy, and they're vital if you need to make a full income. It can seem as if cash flow forecasts at this stage are just guessing games anyway. You're right, they are, so don't let them frighten you. Treat them as a bit of a game, as part of your daydreaming, and they will be more fun. You can be stricter with yourself later down the line once you're comfortable with the idea.

You can customise this one for free on the Wenta business advice website **https://wenta.co.uk** with all the parameters that are relevant to you. For cash/ cheques in, you might put Etsy, PayPal, and Patreon payments, for example. You might write one now which would show you that it's impossible to live on your estimated income. I know that can be very disheartening. After reading this book, maybe doing a couple of courses, you might change your mind completely. The picture might suddenly come into focus and look much more attainable...or the reverse. Whichever is the case, a cash flow forecast is both a snapshot of where you are, and a useful plan for where you want to be. And it really doesn't have to be a chore.

"How can I take money?"

Will you use cash only (which is increasingly disappearing but very useful at fairs)? Or will you take card payments, bank transfers or PayPal? If you take card payments in person, you will need to consider the setup costs of any machinery required.

You do need a payment method for online sales, especially international sales, although most website builders and online marketplaces will make this easy enough to deal with. Etsy, for example, dispatches your earnings directly into your bank account. Whichever you use, account for any fees as part of your expenses, and price accordingly. Incidentally, it could be worth considering your business safety if for any reason you lose access to funds in one single payment platform. You can use more than one platform and let your customers choose. That gives you a backup source of funds if one platform crashes out or you have a major dispute.

If you're an international business, banking methods can sometimes be a great deal slower and fraught with misunderstandings, so PayPal tends to be a good choice. There may be processing fees for business transactions on PayPal, but there are no setup fees and you know what you're getting. There is a certain amount of security throughout the transaction with companies like PayPal, although this isn't always the case with all companies.

Bear in mind that trends in sales and technology are fluctuating and fast-paced, so any information we give you may be out of date within a couple of years. Keep an eye on what's going on in your creative communities, both locally and online.

"Do I need to be insured? What laws relate to my products?"

I am not an expert on this as I have NEVER been fully insured. I simply couldn't afford to be. If I was setting up now, I'd still leave it until I was selling outside a very small circle. You do need to revisit this question when you take each step. Please don't take this as me advising you not to insure! In some cases, it's a legal requirement.

Most very small craft businesses don't need too many bits of paper for a sideline business as long as they aren't producing something that could cause a health hazard. As you grow from just supplying friends, it's a good idea to go to your local government and ask them to point you in the right direction to speak to or contact a small business advisor online. Write a list of concerns you might have or be prepared for questions you think they might ask. Bear in mind if you are producing food or cosmetic items the rules will be a lot stricter a lot sooner in your experiments. Then you need to think about whether your workspace is actually adequate.

Ask yourself: are my products safe? Do my products need to have labels, and what needs to be on the label? If your products are not for children, then you need to state this clearly. You will probably have to look at insurance if there is a chance your product could cause a hazard if badly used. On the other hand, putting all the necessary warnings and aiming at the appropriate market covers you against most problems. Some countries have more litigious systems than others and, in those places, insurance could be considered vital. If you have any concerns, get advice from regional small business advice groups. These are often government funded.

The dreaded taxman

Let's deal with this looming spectre right up front - once it's out of the way you can start to have some fun!

Please note that the rules and regulations may not be exactly as I remember them since I quickly became a "proper" business. And that was a very long time ago. According to my American crafty friends, things are considerably more complicated in the United States, as you need a licence right at the beginning. The exception is selling through Etsy. Etsy deals with the paperwork and pays the taxes for you. You can contact www.sba.gov for advice. I am also told many side hustles are under the table, though I believe in paying tax if you can, as I've stated before. If you follow all the rules when it becomes important to do so, you'll be OK. You can swap a pot of jam for your neighbours' artwork without worrying about tax implications. Just be sensible and don't stress.

You know when you're making a profit, and there are tax rules that can protect you if your craft work is actually loss-making.

The following advice applies to British artists and craftspeople but may also apply to you in principle if you live in other parts of the world. Everything should still be checked with an accountant or business advisor, though. Don't take my word for it!

"I'm just starting out. Surely I don't have to worry about tax?"

No. If you're currently just tinkering around and maybe thinking of trying to sell your work at a fair or two as a side hustle, don't let tax worries put you off getting your first few sales. You can get quite a long way into your experiment without ever earning enough to have any kind of tax liability. But you do need to remember one thing. Even if it's just a vague dream to sell your work, keep receipts for EVERYTHING right from now, and even back in time. If you don't have those old receipts, make a fairly comprehensive list of everything in your craft room or workshop. Note when you bought it and what you paid for it. The tax authority may not take into account anything that you've had more than a year, so concentrate on those things that you've bought in the last year. All your equipment and all your craft supplies, whether you're going to use them instantly or not; all your books and magazines; all your craft classes; your subscriptions to tutorials or to Patreon if you are following other creators for inspiration; your travel costs and entry fees or table fees to relevant craft, miniatures or art fairs, as well as any hotel costs and meals for those events; your posting supplies and any courier costs. Make a separate list of things you use partly for your craft or craft business at home, too. Internet access, for example, and electricity (for your oven, kiln, sewing machine, or any other tools, including your laptop and lighting). Don't push it, just make a fair and honest assessment of the percentage of use. This is all going to add up, I'm sure. You might surprise and even shock yourself how much you did spend over the last year. Then you can add up anything you sold, if you sold anything.

If you can't be bothered with the maths bit, just throw all receipts into a box or file, along with notes, if necessary, to explain what each item was for. Note how it was essential to your business or your business development (such as with professional services and courses). Then you're ready to take a step toward calling your ideas a business. If you don't know where to start, pay an accountant to go through them at the end of a year. The UK government website says this:

"You must send a tax return if, in the last tax year (6 April to 5 April), you were: self-employed as a 'sole trader' and earned more than £1,000 (before taking off anything you can claim tax relief on)"

That's £1,000 not after any deductions. Don't be afraid, though, self-declaration can be easier than you think at a very low income. You need to hang on to the receipts just in case the taxman wants to question you. If you're honest, you don't need to worry about tiny discrepancies. No one is perfect and the tax office doesn't expect you to be superhuman. I made all the mistakes. I over-declared on income and under-declared on costs. But at least I was always more likely to be able to find more costs if the taxman ever came knocking. On the other hand, I know hundreds of extra-small businesses that simply make pocket money and stay under that £1,000 income. And quite a few in the grey area. But I know just as many people who are struggling to get by day-to-day.

My advice about tax if you find you are making a lot of money (which is unusual enough in a craft business), is to simply pay your damn tax and be happy to do so! Lots of people aren't so lucky. But I think 99 out of 100 crafters who sell won't need to pay any extra personal tax if they have a partner who can help to financially support them. They won't have to pay any or a lot of extra tax if they have another job, because you simply can't work enough hours to earn enough above your reasonable costs. But, if you're one of those who does make that big leap, you will at least have developed good habits. If you're successful, you'll be able to pay an accountant to deal with all that mess, because you're unlikely to have the time to do anything more than simply keeping the receipts for someone more competent to deal with. We hope this book helps you into a life where you're paying tax because you can! Whether you like doing it or not.

Now the tax worry is out of the way, I think you may have already spotted the flaw in the plan to go full-time. It's not easy to transition from a hobby to a supremely profitable business. There are ways to make it more profitable though, which we'll discuss later in the book. So, at the beginning you may be working far too hard for far too little to get off the hobby end of the business, into the business end of the hobby. Maybe you just found a way for your hobby to partly pay for itself.

If you really hate working 9-5, and don't mind living frugally (or if you have another reasonably good income coming into the household), it can be a brilliant choice. Especially if you want to be an at-home parent and you need to finance your passion for crafts. If you expect a certain standard of living and you can't take thin months; if there's no other income coming into the household, or if you have big outgoings or responsibilities, then you'll definitely need to have a good long hard think about cutting loose from other employment. But, of course, there'll be a few more ideas to help later. At the time of writing, many people are losing their jobs due to the pandemic. For some people, staying at home, not paying transport or childcare, and being more frugal, can work well. Maybe making a business that pays just under your personal tax allowance could be actually a more relaxed way to live. In the UK, businesses which make under 70 thousand pounds a year don't have to charge, account for, or pay VAT. The drawback is you can't claim back any VAT either.

You can also get advice from government-funded business advice agencies, which are usually free. As for independent business advice companies, such as Wenta, don't be afraid to ask them directly how much they charge for each service. They also have free resources and tutorials.

An American friend of mine shared this useful site with me if you are just starting out in the US: **https://www.sba.gov** The International Revenue Service also has plenty of information that can help you know the rules and **https://europe.mercycorps.org** can give advice to people pulling themselves out of poverty by becoming self-employed. For craft business allowable expenses check out IRS Publication 535.

There is one thing you should definitely bear in mind. Once you convert your hobby into your job, there will be days you despise it as much as any other job, and you have to take responsibility for the fact that it was your choice. Oh yes, I've had to shoulder that knowledge many times. In most of my life, I've hardly worked for anyone else. So my boss is the harshest and once was definitely the lowest paying of all.

However, since I've learned the things we share with you later in the book, I'm all set to have a long tail income into my declining years and Kira is just getting set up to start with a bang, too.

> **Takeaway**: *If you are looking for advice from an accountant or a business advisor, most locations have accountants that advertise themselves as low cost, "working man", or sole traders accountants. They will often give upfront advice free.*

4. Pricing

Valuing both your art and your time

If you have previously only sold as a hobby and have been under-pricing because "it's all just for fun", but things just got serious, the pricing formulas may shock you. So here is my little encouragement to go for what you want, and value not only yourself, but all artists and creators. We have undervalued ourselves for far too long. The world is changing and we are now demanding our dues. I want you to start looking at your value in a different way straight away, before you make the mistake of un-dervaluing your work simply in order to make it more attractive to the cheaper end of the market.

How many people do you know (especially those who are salaried) who would say that they are earning far too much for what they do? Hardly anybody, right? They would all defend their income level by explaining how hard the work is, how long the training or how expensive the investment in their degree or masters or professorship. Everyone, including those who really enjoy their work. Everyone, that is, except artists. A creator almost bows their head and squirms when they ask for their price, no matter what price that is. Very few have grasped the notion of the value of their work, even fewer consider the value of their training and their knowledge. Even those who have learned their art by following others have invested in the books, the courses and the trial and error. Nothing done well is really ever easy. Most of us make art because we love it but, sadly, no matter how hard earned, we see being creative as a privilege and a gift and we allow others to see it that way too.

Think back into prehistory to the place of the artist in their society. I imagine that a gift for constructing pots or carving and engraving wood or stones or making clothing and jewelled pins was much more highly sought after. The creative was an integral part of society just as much as the farmer or the hunter. Later, the decorative artist oiled the wheels of commerce, producing the signs of wealth which every elder and then businessman craved. But when did we decide to devalue the role of artisan? Perhaps it was then when those who created the signs

of wealth along with everyone else became subservient to those who owned it.

"So how does the artist regain that sense of self-worth?"

I could, of course, go into a political rant about how every hour of your time is worth exactly the same amount as messrs Bezos and Zuckerberg, but that doesn't get the job done. So let's start initially by calculation.

Are you now skilled in your craft? Calculate how long your foundation course took, and your degree, if you've become that skilled. This doesn't have to be a real degree, it could be the time you've spent self-teaching. How much has this time earning the minimum cost you in lost wages? And ask yourself whether your skill level in what you do is as great as say a teacher, a banker, a lawyer. Don't ask yourself whether you enjoy the work, most people who have reached a high level in their work derive satisfaction from a job well done. Most of us have days when we really would rather not make that commission, deal with that customer or throw yet another batch of something which didn't work out in the bin. Bankers and accountants enjoy their work too. Some of them don't, but the only reason they don't become artists is because of the low pay. And that's our fault. We have to tell the market what we expect and then the market will decide if we are worth it. If we can't get what we need to live on for what we do then, like anyone else, we need to look at improving our skill level.

We have just been through an extended period (two generations) when real craft work has been increasingly undervalued against fast, plastic, low price, low use and profit. But there is a change happening right now. And right now is where we can grab our place back as creatives in a world suddenly revaluing utility, quality and beauty.

At the moment, however, we are expecting too little for our hard work. But what should we be expecting?

We do seem to demand a kind of humility from artists that we don't expect from high financiers and celebrities. We think that we have to go through a great deal of pain before any gain. That, we think, means pricing our work really low until we get better. But here is why I think that may be the wrong way around. One thing I've seen from artists who do make it, is that they make good art first and the money follows them. The only difference between them and us is that they value their time correctly.

I can give you a real-world example here. My cousin is a doctor. Not a medical doctor, the other sort. She has a good and fairly well-paid job that befits her level of expertise as well as her educational level. And her particular specialisation is ornithology. So, she's a scientist, right? But she is also passionately creative. A few years ago, she started to make beautiful stained-glass representations of her beloved birds and, because that's her field of study, her work is absolutely wonderful. She knows that she knows birds but at first she knew nothing about the business of selling her work. She does now. The reason she was easily able to agree with my advice on pricing was that she was well used to getting a pretty good hourly rate for her work. She knew that her research time had a value and she understood that galleries needed to make pretty massive mark-ups in order to make it worth their while to show her work. She may have had the impostor syndrome as an artist just like the rest of us. But she was a realist and knew if she was going to sell her work and have time to put her very best into it she was very much going to have to count her hours at a massive mark-up and accept another one from the galleries. It simply made mathematical sense to her.

Many of us have never received a proper payment for our value as parents or as artists. The reason for this is very simple. We have never asked for it. We allow ourselves to think we aren't worth it. We're our own worst enemies. Of course, my cousin is paid properly for her wonderful work. People are falling over themselves to buy it, even though the prices are way out of most of our dreams. The result? She works hard...but only when she wants to, and she doesn't have to make anything she's not happy with just to earn a crust. Her work improves as does her value. It's all self-fulfilling and it's all down to not taking part in that self-worth conundrum and the race to the bottom. And what is the difference between you and her? Not that she's inherently a better artist although she might tell me off for saying this. It's that she valued her work logically right from the beginning…Oh, and she is a pretty damn good artist too! This means that if she ever wants to sidestep into full time, she has a firm foundation for a good creative business. This doesn't mean you have to have a doctorate like my cousin does, but you do have to invest in your development and value it. And you also have to rise to your price level.

Well, I'm going to take myself as an example of the top end of craft expertise. Don't be afraid to look at your level dispassionately and don't be afraid of valuing yourself realistically. If, for example, I were working for a large corporation, I could be expecting 40,000 a year for my problem-solving ability. Yes really! No, I have almost never made that amount. Just one year, but that's another story. So that's what I should aim for. And if my husband were to aim for a similar amount, we'd be a lot more able to cope with the slings and arrows. But that's a ridiculously high expectation...isn't it? Well, only until people get it. Of course, we don't. This is only an aim after all. But it isn't a totally unrealistic aim. I do in fact look at 25 euros an hour, but for 50% of my hours I'm not making. I'm marketing, or writing, or inventing tools. And in my husband's case there is some making of the craft tools but most of his hours are spent on admin.

Even If you only expect 15 an hour of your standard working week, your prices will be much higher than you think. If you don't get and work on this basic premise, I can promise you your work won't rise in price or value because you are too busy trying to work quickly to have time to work carefully or to give yourself development time.

Pricing formulas

How you can work out what you need to charge by 'hours plus.' There is the other "what the market can stand" calculation, but this is the absolute bottom line. You shouldn't even consider going below this.

Most craftspeople are not naturally incredibly mathematically able, and so I'm going to assume that you, like me, are not very comfortable with theoretical maths or algebra. I'll break it down into its easiest addition and subtraction (with a little multiplication and division on a calculator or spreadsheet). And let's not be afraid of paying for a couple of hours of an accountant's time to help when we get towards making anything more substantial or official. Let me say straight away that if you calculate properly, your prices will probably have to be much higher than you first imagined. And if you've been happily buying cheap, mass produced crafts for a while, the true value of your work may surprise you.

Let me explain why you can't possibly sell

that pendant which took you an hour to make, for a fiver plus the cost of material (the way most craftspeople initially look at pricing). Quite apart from the fact that a fiver an hour is ridiculous even if you do love what you do.

Divide your required monthly income by how many hours you can comfortably work per month to get a gauge of your total hourly profit needed. So, I know you are going to work more than this but let's say that you have a 35 hour working week. Comfortable, right? You can exchange more of your hours for more money if you like. This is just for the sake of the argument about what you're worth. So this is all the hours you work a week on everything. This is to be added to your costs, both fixed and per item produced. Normally the time element of any craft work will be the largest 'cost', unless of course you are working with items such as precious metals or stones.

So let's say for the sake of argument that you want to earn around £25,000 per year. Try and keep yourself just under the higher tax rate and, in the UK, the VAT rate. This means you are going to be looking at 16.29 per hour if you work an average of 35 productive hours a week and award yourself 8 weeks of holiday and or sick pay. The maths bit 46 (weeks a year) Into 25,000 pounds makes 568 per week you need to earn to get to your target yearly figure. 35 hours into 568 means 16.29 per working hour.

I can almost hear you crying "Wow, 8 weeks holiday?! I think this is an unrealistic hope for most workers - most are lucky to get 4 weeks annual leave!" and "Is 35 hours a week realistic? Isn't the average working week around 40 hours, or more? I think self-employed people often work even harder than that!"

I can hear it from you because this is exactly what Kira has just said.

I'm going to answer that very simply.

You can work harder for less money if you want.

Think of me as that unusual creature, the benevolent employer. And if you don't want to burn out, end up sick with no fall back or unable to get over the hump of a slow period, you will value your hours properly. And then... more hours, more money, right? Don't work out your required income

on the basis of expecting to be overworking, please.

I'm not telling you exactly what your work is worth. I'm telling you how to think about it.

How am I so sure I'm right? Because I got it wrong for myself. Since then, I've given this formula out to several artists who have proved its worth over and over.

"So we said 16.29 a working hour? Does this mean the pendant is now priced at 16.29?"

No, I'm afraid it's not that simple.

You need to take into account that, as a small business owner, not all your hours are productive. A significant amount will be spent researching, learning, planning, buying, marketing and selling. Maybe even

cleaning your workshop. After all, you're the skivvy too, aren't you? Maybe only 50% of your time will be spent actually producing your stock. Don't forget to add these hours. This means you would have to double your productive hour cost in your pricing calculations. Let's say, for example; you're making a batch of flower pendants and it takes an average of 60 minutes for the whole process. That means you need to charge 2 x 1 hour of your time. a whole 2 hours at 16.29... plus manufacturing costs, plus sales costs (that market stall fee wasn't cheap was it?), plus a proportion of fixed costs. Your cash flow forecast helps you identify your fixed and variable costs. That's coming up. For now, just put an estimate of your fixed costs in. Then you have to take off sales tax plus income tax before you can get a total yearly, monthly or averaged-out hourly income. After all this, your pendant may well have a value of well over 30 pounds. This is probably twice what you thought you might charge for it at the top end and look how little those costs really fall, even if you treat yourself like a zero-hours worker.

> **Top tip**: Don't get confused if an accountant or bank manager starts asking you "Is that gross or net". Gross profit and net profit are two different things. Gross is before any taxation. Net is after. The same with gross and net income. Which for a sole trader is near enough the same thing. Just make sure you know the difference.

you want to earn that per hour. So you may want to add on what you would be prepared to take back off the retail price to make sure you always get at least your hourly minimum. Wholesale prices can be anything from 20% off to 50% off but I wouldn't go to that top end unless your products are mass produced or at least easily home produced with faster production line style methods. For example, my craft materials (sticks of polymer clay foods for slicing) and my crafter tools (moulds and stencils) are reproducible quickly and in higher quantities so they do attract a high discount for trade. But your daisy pendant can't be reproduced especially if you labelled it OOAK

FEAR-FREE PRICING CALCULATION - FOR RIGHT BRAINED CRAFTERS

Pricing #1 Hourly rate calculation. The difficult bit first

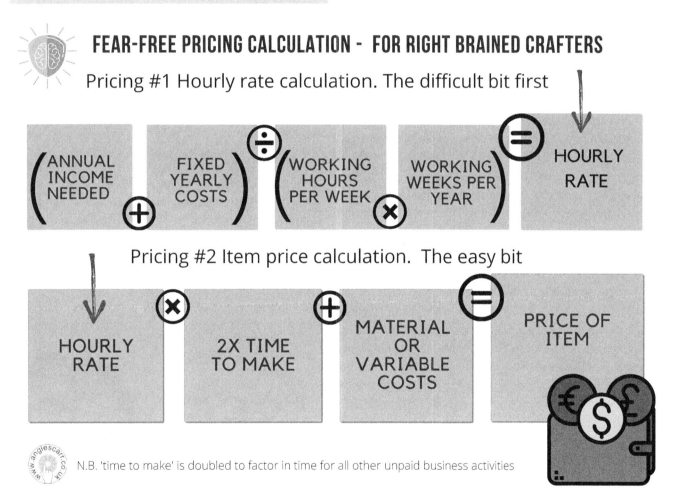

$$(\text{ANNUAL INCOME NEEDED} + \text{FIXED YEARLY COSTS}) \div (\text{WORKING HOURS PER WEEK} \times \text{WORKING WEEKS PER YEAR}) = \text{HOURLY RATE}$$

Pricing #2 Item price calculation. The easy bit

$$\text{HOURLY RATE} \times \text{2X TIME TO MAKE} + \text{MATERIAL OR VARIABLE COSTS} = \text{PRICE OF ITEM}$$

N.B. 'time to make' is doubled to factor in time for all other unpaid business activities

You're self-employed. No sick pay for you! If you're in the States, no health insurance either. Unless you have lots of money for insurance to pay for these protections. Oh, and no pension payments unless you factor that in or find another way of ensuring a constant income. Bear with me. This is still the minimum price you need to ask. And, hang-on…what about if you want to sell wholesale and you need to sell at a discount? Well then you have to aim for an even higher retail price to discount against! My pricing guide shows the minimum price you can ask if

(One of a Kind) so the trade customer is just going to have to pay what you want and will have to slap a hefty premium on top in his gallery or shop for owning this unique treasure.

Top tip about unconsidered benefits from selling to the trade: remember that wholesale sales actually do add a plus to your figures. I don't want to go too deeply into this but let's put it this way. The utility of passing on most of the marketing and sales costs to the wholesaler customer does have a value. They can deal with the demanding customers and some of the marketing for you. Plus, they are actually something of a free marketing resource for you. The prestige of being in their shop may work for you too. Some of these trade customers only choose the best. And they chose you! I have heard some artists actually complain about these retailers actually having the cheek to price up their work to double! Well guys, they are doing you a favour. Be nice to them. They have an eye for the cool and unusual. They are prepared to give valuable shop space and marketing time to your goods. The value they create is theirs. It also has a knock-on effect on the way your public sees you and the way you see your own value. Cherish them!

Does your re-jigging of these sums look like what you need per year or per month? If it's not, you need to adjust and keep adjusting. If you have never applied the cash flow forecast to your household income it might be a good time to do that too. Remember, if you want to be self-employed, you might have to apply some seriously frugal principles to your life until you get right off the ground. If you can't do that maybe better to stay with a regular paycheck. You will be adjusting down and up and maybe sometimes down again throughout your craft business life.

And this is why you can't make a pendant which takes an hour for a fiver. Does this make sense? So now you see why my previous advice is never to price low. Pricing low is a race to the bottom and a sure-fire way of scuppering your burgeoning business before it starts and hammering yourself into a position where you can't grow either as a business or as an artist. Now you know this, there are several things you can do if the item doesn't seem worth that price. You can choose to practise hard enough that your work is such good quality that nobody will question that price, or you can find ways of speeding up production. Remember, my formula assumes that you sell everything you make, so don't be afraid of the higher prices to cover that eventuality that something doesn't sell. But do always value your time at a serious rate, whatever level of business you are in.

After that you can look at what the market will stand. And that's a whole other step up the scale of a successful business!

There may also be other incomes not from sales (such as royalties from books and payments for classes) to be taken into account in your timetable, but we'll deal with these possible income sources and how they can affect your current and future incomes later in the book. For now, let's concentrate on pitching your product at the higher price end.

If you are going to be selling on Etsy, you can find Etsy pricing calculators online. These can help give you an idea of what your pricing should be in a few clicks, taking into account the cost of materials, fees and hours taken to make your product. It's not as complex as a full business plan, but if yours is just a hobby they are better than nothing.

Cash flow forecast

"Isn't this the wrong way around in the book, shouldn't it have come before pricing?"

Well yes, it should. But would you have read any further if it had?

While you are working out this pricing you will already be halfway to a cash flow forecast. You may as well get right down to this guessing game straight away. Then you can feed the figures back into your pricing calculations. This will generate the numbers you need to try out for your fixed costs. You can add any major expenses into your formula too for now as fixed costs, although an accountant will deal with them a little differently. Don't be afraid of the cash flow forecast. My advice is to think of it as just a bit of fun at first. You can do as many of these as you like and they can be as wildly optimistic or pessimistic as you like, in the first instance. After all this is just an exercise for you. You aren't presenting it on Dragon's Den!

Here is our friend **Countess Bascula**. She loves sewing and costuming. Her friends loved her corsets and asked her to make some for them. She's just lost her job as a phlebotomist working in pandemic test and trace, now that there's a vaccine. Please forgive me my bad first edition joke.

She thinks she might have a chance in business. But although she shares her house to minimise outgoings, she doesn't have a partner, business or otherwise, to support her so she needs to do the maths.

Everyone who wants to go full time needs a cash flow forecast and the countess is no exception. Of course she loves to count (and weigh and measure), whereas a lot of us hate it, so we've simplified the concept for you. Yours may look very different and will be a lot more complex. You can find free downloadable cash flow forecasts online (such as the one on www.wenta. co.uk). They can be a bit more complicated than this one. There are many other free cash forecast programs, or you can simply use a spreadsheet. You could also ask an accountant to design one for you which does the sums. Just a quick explanation of what some of the columns mean. All the lines marked A are income and all those marked B are outgoings. To know how much money you've added to the business at the end of each month you take the total of A lines and then take away the total of the B lines. Income minus expenses and drawings. In this case we have taken out month zero, because there wasn't space, and just put 500 in the opening bank line, as if our business owner started out with 500, say from her last pay cheque. Oh, and I should explain the difference between income and drawings too. Income is all of your takings. Drawings is how much money you take out as your wages. You can see in our example that the countess wants to be frugal but needs to take out 750 of her profits just to survive, and she thinks she should try to leave 35 in each month to try to build her business, or incase she has a big expense like sewing machine repair.

Your cash forecast is just for you, at least at first. It's important because it gives you an idea where you are now and where you're going. If your monthly income is your only income then it's super important you know whether you're going to come crashing down in the near or distant future so that you can adjust your outgoings, your sales and of course your expectations when you need to. It also helps you understand how much you need to earn which in turn helps you set your pricing. If you aren't part of a family group where someone else can take the strain, in a bad month you have to be very aware how this will affect you going forward. So a cash flow forecast isn't a one-time thing. It's something you might want to go back and back to. You don't need to do it yourself if you can get someone else to do it for you, but you do need to understand what it is and why these numbers can affect your success or failure. You can have a loss-making month, or even a year if you have some money put aside to keep you afloat. If you're down to your last fiver and you can't afford your materials, then you're in trouble.

Let's look at the various parts in their simplest forms. Money-in can be income or it can be borrowings. It can be from many different sources, and you can separate these out once you get comfortable with these forecasts. For now you're likely to be just guessing, and that's fine..

The countess thinks she can make 2 boned corsets a night, if she works all night four nights a week. An extra day to catch up when she gets behind. She's been selling each for 50 pounds/dollars/euros plus Etsy's cut. Her postage costs are around 10 dollars/pounds/euros (bear with me, we aren't going to carry on explaining that this applies to all the possible currencies).

She's declaring part of her rent as a business cost, since she uses a room which she could have otherwise rented out for 400. The trouble is that out of her apparently large turnover of nearly 23,000 per year, when she's taken out her costs, she's earning a paltry 9,000. Barely enough to keep body and soul together, let alone buy a new deluxe coffin to sleep in! She doesn't even know what the taxman wants from her yet, and so she's just put down what she thinks national insurance might cost. If she lived in Spain her national insurance payment would be 3,000 per year, so it's a good job she lives in Transylvania isn't it? Of course, she's written these figures down off the top of her head. She's not happy. She remembers there are only 12 hours a night at best and sometimes only 8. She hasn't taken account of the hours she will need to spend on marketing. After looking at these and considering what she thinks she really needs to earn, she knows that she's going to have to change her prices dramatically and perhaps bring in another type of income in case sales are slow one month. She has to cover her fixed costs every month!

These calculations are massively simplified but do give you an idea.

She has several options. She can give up right now and go and get another job, keeping her hobby as a sideline, or she has to have a radical rethink.

Well, let's imagine she has read this book, especially the pricing formula which she's now put up on her wall.

Simplified Cashflow Forecast Ms C Bascula

Income		Month 1	Month 2	Month 3	Extrapolated to year end
A	Etsy	900	900	900	10,800
A	Website	1,000	1,000	1,000	12,000
A	Total	1,900	1,900	1,900	22,800
Money out - fixed costs		Month 1	Month 2	Month 3	Extrapolated to year end
B	Rent and rates	400	400	400	4,800
B	Gas and electricity	75	75	75	900
B	Telephones and internet	15	15	15	180
Money out - variable costs		Month 1	Month 2	Month 3	Extrapolated to year end
B	Materials	320	320	320	3,840
B	Postage and stationery	280	280	280	3,360
B	Tax and national insurance	25	25	25	300
B	Personal drawings	750	750	750	9,000
B	Total	1,865	1,865	1,865	22,380
Results		Month 1	Month 2	Month 3	Extrapolated to year end
A-B	Money in - out	35	35	35	420
	Opening bank	500	535	570	885
	Closing bank	535	570	605	920

She's also been to a therapist to help get rid of her artist impostor syndrome. And she's looked through our alternative income section and she has had a few new ideas.

Her corsets are now double the price. Of course, she sells fewer, but she can make them better and add more details, and she's enjoying it more because it's not so rushed. She's found that spending more time means her customers see the difference and have started talking about how precise her work is and how wonderful her customer service. She's found a night a week to blog about costume design and she's gaining a bit of a cult following. She's been asked to make outfits for a gothic celebrity wedding. So she's now got a waiting list for her corsets and has been able to ask an even higher price for them. She's also decided to sell PDFs of her patterns because she has so many bright ideas while she's sleeping. She's releasing a pattern a month. And making another couple of hundred a month from them. People love her quirky style and want to know what she's up to next, so she has a Patreon page to share tips and tricks with supporters who are now happy to pay three dollars each a month, and she has 100 patrons.

Now she can afford to take a holiday, be sick, and buy the silk bedding she had her eye on. And her customers don't quibble because her work is so good. She has small but building income streams to provide for the future and she's considering writing a book on costuming. All because she doubled her prices! Why was she so afraid of that?

This is why pricing properly from the very beginning isn't scary at all. It makes absolute economic sense.

Try some cash flow forecasting yourself. You can use the figures in your pricing formula.

Takeaway: *Don't be afraid of numbers (I actually am a bit, but shh, don't tell anyone!). Just tell yourself it's playing, and it really is! Play a lot! Give yourself a week of playing if necessary. At first it may seem as if it's daunting to get from your first unrealistic ideas but the more you play... the more you learn.*

5. Market research

"What is it and why should I do it?"

Market research is a vital process to help you understand how to shape your business. This includes taking a look at what is already on the market, and who your target customers are. Some of the information and the searching practise you pick up will assist you later. Take notes! It's not a big frightening subject. It's just taking a long hard look at the business you are thinking of going into, and where you think you might fit in. Even if you've already started selling, it's never too late to go back and do some market research exercises again. In fact, if you want your business to have longevity, then you will want to continually stay on top of what's going on in your industry.

The first thing to do is find out whether your product is totally unique. If it is, then you're in a great deal of luck, as your originality will stand out. The negative, however, could be that people don't understand the concept. The chances are that there is something around that is at least similar to or related to your product. Don't worry, you can still enter the market even if what you make is something that hundreds of other people already sell. Just ask yourself what you can provide that is original.

Ask yourself whether you are making this item because you want to be creative or because you need the money. If you need the money, you really can't afford to make the same number of mistakes as a hobby crafter does, so you need to get a clear idea of market saturation and price levels.

"What if someone else is already making what I make, and it's very cheap?"

Unless you want to join the race to the bottom, you really need to be offering something different in terms of design, quality and 'heart'. Heart is that special something that makes people want to buy from you even if they can get the same product cheaper elsewhere. It's a very useful ability to be a 'customer whisperer', however, even very lovely people can starve when money is tight. So, being lovely is an asset but it can't be your only asset. You do need at least two of the above three points. You can get away with two if you can build on them. If you have all three then you could be on to a winner.

Ask yourself "do I have more ideas up my sleeve?". You can start with just one, but you may need to consider the lifespan of your one idea. Even when quality and heart are always in your work, if your first idea has been taken or copied, goes out of fashion or you've mined the market, how easy will it be for you to move on to another project? If you've only just started and you aren't in a rush to decide, all this will come to you organically. But if you're suddenly unemployed and you need to know whether to spend a redundancy cheque on craft supplies, this might be the time to do some serious market research.

You can begin to research simply by typing into Google the main words that describe your product and seeing what comes up in the first few results pages. You can do the same thing with social media, too. Many of the things you find out during this process will be very useful when you are developing your marketing. Researching the key terms and phrases surrounding your business will help a lot with choosing the right product names and descriptions for selling your work online. Kira will teach you the importance of keyword research for product descriptions later on, so keep notes to help you then, or you can always skip to Chapter 10.

See if there is something similar on the market and then start looking at your nearest competitors. What are they doing that you like (or don't like)? What price levels are they charging? Try to get an idea of how popular they actually are, such as by looking at sales figures and reviews on Etsy, and their social media following. As well as looking online, visit craft fairs and take notes. See who is selling well - which stands are regularly surrounded by customers? Are they doing something that attracts you? Which stands do you walk straight by, and why? Instead of being put off by other successful businesses in your field, be motivated by them - particularly if you think you can add something extra.

You could test the market a little by asking your friends what they feel they would pay for a similar product if it wasn't yours. Ask them to be honest. Ask them if there's any reason they would choose your product apart from the fact it's yours. Mostly our friends will say no because they are too used to getting art for free. But some will happily pay the going rate. Look back at my most important piece of advice about pricing. This is, from my point of view, the absolute crux of the book. And don't under-price your work for friends either. I have two friend prices. The proper price...or free. Of course, friends will ask for a discount but only ever drop the price if you need the money and you know they're only buying to help you out.

As well as looking at who your competitors are, you really need to get a good handle on who your customers are and why they might want to buy your product over a similar item produced by a competitor. Your customers are what your success will depend on, so you want to understand what makes them tick. When looking at marketability, it's difficult to know whether to look at your product or your customer first because these ideas are very closely connected. A bit like how a successful novel author may either write wonderful stories and then find the customers for them, or may find the customers and "write to market". That is to say, write stories that they know their readers will enjoy. It's the same with any product You make it, people like it, and so you sell it. Or, people like similar things...so you identify a niche and make it your own. A good balance is to make the thing that works for you, that you enjoy, but apply tweaks that make it inherently desirable for your customers - for example when you identify a gap in the market that you can fill.

Don't rush the market research and planning part because, if you do, you will probably end up throwing time and money down the drain. One really great thing about being in a truly creative business where you are spending time making repeat items is that you have 'musing' time. If you grab a notebook and have it next to you while you're creating, you can usually find yourself musing about these questions and having some great (and of course some not so great) ideas for your product development and marketing strategy. I say some not-so-great ideas because we all come up with immediate inspirations which seem good at the time but on reflection aren't so great and maybe involve spending a lot of money for an uncertain outcome. If you note it down, however, you will know when your idea is truly inspired because it will excite you at the time and it will still excite you a week later when you look at it again.

Market research and marketability exercise:

Get your notebook and answer these questions for yourself. You'll use many of these later when thinking about branding. In each case compare these values to those of your competitors. Are you offering anything in each of these areas? Are you offering something with a greater quality or value?

Incidentally, your 'competitors' may also be your friends. As long as you're offering something that's different, it doesn't hurt to discuss your ideas with them. Most crafters are supportive of each other except if you're treading directly on their turf by copying, which is a no-no, or by sucking away their customers directly from their shop or stand. Most crafters will appreciate that a superb artist in an exhibition/magazine or selling group will attract customers for all of them. However, undercutting with lower prices on similar products would also get most crafters a little upset.

1. What am I making that's original? If there is something similar on the market, what sets mine apart from the competitors?

2. Who is my audience?

3. Who am I to them?

4. What are my values?

5. Is my personality visible in my work?

6. Do people want to talk about my work?

7. Will I still enjoy making this item if I have to make a thousand of them? If the answer is no, put up the price! If it's a dramatic no, put up the price dramatically.

8. Do I want to sell OOAK (one of a kind) works?

If you have answered Yes to number eight, you may not want to teach. If not:

9. Do I have a technique, a tool, etc. to sell alongside my work?

10. Do I want to, and could I, teach my work?

11. Can I write good instructions?

9 10 and 11 are important in my business but may not be in yours. These are just a starting point and will hopefully inspire you to come up with more questions to be investigated.

It really helps to have a very clear idea where your business is going, and where you place yourself in the market. It's never too late to go back and look at these questions again, especially if you suddenly find you have too much or too little work. At this point you may need to ask yourself "Do I want my business to grow, or am I happier with a simple one-person business with no pressure?". At some point you are going to have to make a decision about your direction. You should look at this sooner rather than later, as it may well affect your marketing strategy.

By the way, I don't want you to think that pressure is always bad because sometimes you can do your very best work under pressure. How many of us in the business have got right up to the wire for a fair, exhibition or product launch? Then we resented the fact that we've just had a fabulous idea which we just don't have time to put into practise. Stress can sometimes trigger the best inspiration.

One more thing for this very condensed look at market research. Don't only look at the people's work that you love, especially if you're aiming to make something different. Take a good look at the work you hate. Why do you dislike it so much? What would/could you improve? How would your work 'wow' people when their work doesn't 'wow' you? I would say it's even more helpful to look at what you don't like in the current market and go in another direction than it is to follow the people whose work is already highly regarded. Now you know what you've got. Time to tell the public how wonderful it is.

> **Takeaway**: *If you work out what is wonderful about your product and pin it down. If you do this before you have a chance to let the insecurity gremlins in, you will find it infinitely easier to sell those ideas and those products to the world. Do your market research and look at your competitors. Get a firm understanding of what you need to do to compete - then move on and do your own thing!*

Finding your customers and connecting with them

"Who would buy my work?"

One of the first questions to ask when assessing your business is "who is my customer?" The answer to this can change throughout your working life, but it can affect what you sell and how you market it.

A great starting exercise for your working 'musing time' is to imagine yourself making the item that you are currently making for your favourite customer. Who are they and what makes them your favourite? Then write about him/her as if you were writing a character for a novel. Do it even if it feels silly...until it feels silly and even a bit more. You can then give him/her a name. Let's call my customer Bea (Bea good customer - get it?!). My favourite customer is patient because she loves my work and knows I'm going to take a little more time than Amazon to get it to her. She's not rich but will pay for what she wants without question. Your favourite customer may well be extremely rich...ours aren't. My favourite customer is also a maker herself and so she understands the value of the tools and materials I produce to make her life easier. But she also buys and resells (and sometimes keeps for herself) my products. My favourite customer will respond to my calls to buy on special offer when I need a quick injection of cash flow. Now let's get silly. She's 50 years old. Her children have grown up. She's pretty and has dimples when she laughs.

Why did I do the silly bit? Because I want to humanise my imaginary customer, and feel that she's a lovely person who deserves my very best work. This helps me remember to put more love into my work and never to sell anything to 'her' (all of my customers) that's poor quality. I don't always get that right, but it's a great aim.

If you've already started selling online, you can gather analytics on your shop's activity. Using analytics gives you plenty of hard data on who your customers are, where they're from and how they've found you. More on that later in the "Measuring your marketing performance" Chapter 14.

Once you've found your ideal customers, you need to learn how to connect with them. Connecting with them is a major part of marketing. We'll cover various aspects of marketing separately in the following chapters, as it's a big subject. For now, just remember to do your market research, and this will inform how you connect with your customer when you begin marketing.

6. Marketing: the first steps

"Hang on, isn't marketing just a fancy word for selling?"

No, "sales" refers to all the things involved in actually selling your work. This could include booking and preparing for and going to fairs and the process of wrapping up the items and taking the money. There is a bit of a crossover with marketing at the point of sale where you are actually talking to your customers about your pieces, displaying advertising information, handing out business cards, leaflets and free samples, and that sort of thing. This counts as marketing, because the act of marketing is the process of getting people aware and interested enough to want to buy from you, and encouraging them to spread that interest. The love of your public is quite simply free advertising and it's also the very best advertising because it's scattering the seed on the most fertile ground. Most craftspeople are naturally likeable. Your customers feel that and love to share it around. Also, people like to be your friend and your 'discoverer.' Make it easy for them. And whenever possible, show that you appreciate the free and kind publicity work they do for you.

A lot of marketing talk may sound like corporate jargon at first but, put simply, what it means to us is planning, and putting into action, all the ways you're going to encourage people to buy your work. When it comes to selling and bringing in customers, remember that marketing is equal in importance to designing and making your products. Neither can work without the other.

"But why is marketing so important?"

Look at the market research you've done as part of the previous chapter and take stock of your current position in the market. If you've been selling for a while, where are you at the moment? Review what you think you have done well so far and what is holding you back. Now might be the time to write up where you are and where you'd like to be in the market. You could be one of the least known. Or not very well known...yet. Maybe, like I was a few years ago, one of the best known...but not making any money.

The problem could be your marketing. Perhaps, like me at that time, you're not marketing the right thing or in the right way. Awareness doesn't necessarily lead to sales. Being well-known is lovely but if it doesn't put bread on your table it's just window dressing on a closed shop. So, to get you started, here is a brief list of areas that fall under the umbrella term of 'marketing'.

- *Developing a brand identity*
- *Developing and advertising your unique selling points*
- *Online marketing, including social networking, blogging or guest posting on blogs, communicating with influencers, using paid ads and improving search engine optimisation (aka SEO)*
- *Offline marketing, including leaflets, magazines, features on TV, radio and podcasts*
- *Promotions, special offers and discounts*
- *Attending and organising events (online and offline)*

We discuss the nuts and bolts of online marketing, including basic SEO, in the "Improving your online sales" section a bit later on, along with social media marketing. If you're going for the big time or even only want to make an adequate living, these days you can't afford to miss those bits out. Other forms of marketing, such as both free and paid advertising methods are explained in the relevant chapters.

"How do I start planning my marketing strategy? I'm not even sure what a marketing strategy is!"

Developing a marketing strategy refers to breaking down your ideas and goals into small, achievable steps. You need to look at the short term, medium term and long term, and also to divide your marketing goals up into the most important tasks. Since you can't do everything at once it can be best to pick them off one by one in order of importance. Bear in mind that you want to plan on having some high-value, high-importance marketing activity planned. Prepared work you can keep putting out throughout the year, particularly if you're looking at the long term. Start to make lists of what you need to learn in order to make it possible to do each of these things. A strategy can be a complex set of interconnecting tasks to reach out to your customers and then bring them closer and closer to buying from you. This is sometimes called a funnel. I like to think I'm less cynical than that but if you want to be successful, you have to plan. Your customers don't know where you are or what you stand for until you tell them.

"What are the benefits of learning all of this and handling it for myself?"

While you can hire people to assist with your marketing, the benefit of taking a DIY approach is that it allows you to stay in charge of what you do and how much you spend, and to understand the costs and benefits. Plus, you won't be ripped off if you end up deciding to hire the help in.

I have a mantra which I use when making my miniature polymer clay items: "simplify and exaggerate." I think this can be applied to marketing and advertising your products. I don't mean you should literally exaggerate anything. Just that you should focus on the essence of what you are trying to say and say it as simply and clearly as possible. This is not necessarily something I find easy and so it's a mantra worth keeping in mind even when writing books like this one! Fortunately, my co-writer Kira is much better at keeping on point when writing copy. This is something I need to learn. So, recognising the things that you need to learn ahead of time and investing in them is an important part of planning your marketing and what you can do.

Building your brand

So you've developed your products to a sellable point, you've done a little market research, you may have already calculated your costs and worked out your prices, and you're now feeling ready to attend physical events, set up an online shop, or approach retailers. This is a great time to work on your brand and branding, so that you can infuse your business with some personality and give it life.

We've mentioned your personality as one of your unique selling points in the market research section. Now is the time to develop the personality into a brand identity. The aim of developing strong branding is to increase brand awareness through your marketing. The stronger your branding, the more memorable you are, and the more people will be aware of your brand. The more brand awareness you have can help to dictate your position in the market. If your brand is likeable and memorable, then you have a higher chance of success.

Let's take a step back and clarify what we're talking about. Rather than just being your product or company name, a brand encompasses company and product image/identity, ethos, customer experience and any other unique factors that make yours different from other brands. It is the face and story of your company and it is a marketing tool.

Branding, on the other hand, is the act of building your brand and reinforcing your brand messaging, taking into account the above factors, as well as involving the strategy with which you do it. A large part of branding involves creating a cohesive corporate visual identity and reflecting this in all aspects of business.

Branding can take many forms. These include:

- *Company name*
- *Logo design*
- *Packaging*
- *Writing style*
- *Colour scheme*
- *Website design*
- *Product design*
- *Advertising type and style*
- *Other visual imagery (such as on social media)*

Of course, a really good product can speak for itself, and you may find success without considering this step at all. Nevertheless, a strong brand can be more memorable and appear more reputable to customers. Well-considered branding will help you to get a firm foothold in your market and help you to have a better connection with customers. Ultimately with the aim of building a loyal customer base.

Regardless of any measurable business benefits, brand-building is one of the most enjoyable parts about starting a business! After all, it's a chance to let your creativity loose a little. We've devised some fun writing exercises to help kickstart your thinking about ways that you can create a solid brand and branding strategy for your new business which instantly tells the world what you're all about.

Branding exercises:

1. What are you like as a person? Outgoing? Introverted? Wild? Political? Colourful? Funny? Pessimistic? Come up with at least 3 adjectives to describe yourself, but don't stop there if you can think of more.

You might be thinking "but I don't want my brand to reflect me as a person!". That's fine. You may wish to keep your personal life and identity private, or you may be shy and retiring while making exaggerated or revealing costumes that you would never wear yourself. That's ok! This is just a prompt to get you thinking about how you come across and what kind of persona you want to build your business with.

It's worthwhile to remember too, when you are engaging in marketing and outreach, that customers do sometimes like to see the face behind the craft. You may need to tweak your public face to suit your business at times, but it's wise to consider these things in advance to ensure you are projecting the image you want to. Also, bear in mind that any image you project needs to appear consistent and authentic. So don't try to be something you're not. On the other hand, sometimes you have to channel your more outgoing or confident self when you pick up the phone or appear in public. Stage fright? Fake it until you make it, as they say.

2. What are your personal unique selling points as a business owner, Not just your products but your service delivery. What do you do differently from others in your category? What are you able to offer your customers that other businesses don't? From bespoke product options to customer service, there's a lot of space here to identify what you can do that is special. And, of course, use what you've identified that the rest of the market does badly. For example, perhaps you are the only one who adds flower scents to your flower posies, or the only one in your field to offer a gift wrapping and tagging service. If you're in a crowded market, these touches are even more important.

Once you know what these things are, you can highlight them in your branding and marketing, and work on making them an integral part of your brand identity.

3. Is there a problem that you're trying to solve with your work? This is a really important question as it will form part of the core of your marketing. What annoys you? What do you want to see more or less of in your field? How does your product or service address these problems?

Not every business needs to lead with a manifesto, but if you can outline a gap in the market in terms of a problem you want to solve, this can help you to position yourself correctly, and build your brand ethos.

4. What are your favourite colour schemes? Do these correspond with the norm for other businesses in your sector? Do you want to fit in with those busi-

nesses, or do you want to stand out and do something completely different?

When considering your branding strategy, it's also useful to think about where you can build consistency and recognisability in your branding, and colour scheme is a great place to start. You can use the same colour palette in multiple places to get that consistency. Examples include in your logo, on your packaging, stall coverings and on your website.

When choosing your brand colour scheme, it's helpful to imagine it in various contexts. Ask yourself if it will be readable and appealing on your website (more about this in website dos and don'ts). Will this colour grouping remind people of other products you don't want to be associated with? Take your time before investing too much into an unsuitable colour scheme. For example, you might not want a health product to carry the same colours as a fast food brand.

5. What are your values as a business-owner? A big part of what forms a brand are the abstract values associated with it. If you can't think of what your business values might be off the top of your head, take a look at the list below, and circle or write down the ones that are applicable to your business. Or add your own. There are no wrong answers!

Affordable	*Feminine*	*Friendly*	*Apolitical*
Exclusive	*Masculine*	*Trustworthy*	*Luxurious*
High-end	*Gender-neutral*	*Funny*	*Complex*
Practical	*Political*	*Inclusive*	*Simple*

6. What is the story of your brand? How did it come to be? Storytelling is a strong part of branding and building an identity. Try writing a brief biography as it relates to this brand, say, a paragraph or two. How would you tell someone you first met in a lift or a queue who you are and what your business is about in just one minute? How will you get them from not knowing you at all to saying "Oh really? Tell me more". Don't waste time on "my name is". Start with "I'm". It's much more powerful and confident. At first you might find this exercise difficult, especially if you are humble or introverted, but being proud of what you do and refining your bio can help get rid of any uncertain moments in the future. It also helps you to focus on your own direction and distil your brand identity down to a few words. If you have difficulty with branding you can buy in help with this. It could make a serious difference to your confidence in presenting yourself and your product.

Give yourself a name that people recognise.

Have you chosen a name? Is it your actual name or a 'purely business' name? This may be more important than ever in the digital age. Either way, it has to be memorable.

I have a friend who actually I haven't seen for some time. She was very well known by her actual name because her work is very beautiful. Unfortunately, she had a very long and complicated business name "Miniature something, something, and something else". I can't now even remember what the last word was, which may just show the problem of such a long business name. Additionally, she has recently remarried. Bear in mind that the issue of name changes can be a big problem for married women in business.

If your business has you and your creativity as its unique selling point, it's not egotistical to use and advertise your own name. And it's not egotistical to keep a name in spite of a changed marital status. It's good business. If you feel uncomfortable with that, choose an artist pseudonym you feel comfortable with and can stick to. You'll have to live with it forever or lose your greatest brand investment.

A double name strategy halves the impact. You then have to spend twice as much money or time or both making sure that the world knows who you are and what you do. If you are a reseller, your business name simply needs to be attractive and memorable. When your art is straight from the heart, you could use a punchy business name, but even so I think it should connect straight back to you. as those who use part of their name in their business title do seem to do better in social media marketing. There are names in this world that just jump out. One is Fanniminiature. She has linked her name to the descriptive 'miniature', always using this instead of her very long full name. This and her absolutely wonderful work, helps her build a successful online presence. Also, who can fail to notice that her name is pretty memorable to English speakers, especially Brits!

Having said all this, if you have two separate businesses it can be a good idea to have a separate name, especially if the worlds would clash. I have recently brought a book out under a pseudonym because I don't want people con-fusing my very gentle and calm world of miniatures with my rather crabby old lady writing personality. However, I know that promoting that book will be a real uphill battle because I quite simply have to start all over again marketing the "new" writing personality. Personality is really important for small businesses, and potentially even more important in the crafting world. You may have picked up on this in the branding exercises, but I can't stress this enough: personality sells.

A note on politics, religion and prudery

I admit, I don't always follow the very good advice about not letting politics and religion creep into your brand. For better or worse, that's part of my personality. If Billy Bragg hadn't been into politics, where would he have been as a musician? He has a brand that works for him and he wouldn't change that to appeal to a right-wing crowd. Banksy is almost a non-personality, like a shady, anti-hero character. There aren't many people who can get away with mixing controversy and branding. But if you can and it's what makes you, perhaps you should. It is possible that you will be cutting off your fluffy bunny market in favour of your growling wolf market. But if it's absolutely who you are, and you know your niche, then go for it. You may be a painter of erotic images, for example. You can't afford to let people's prudery affect your exploring of your art. But there is one caveat: you must be prepared to take the flak without getting overly defensive. You must avoid deliberately antagonising your potential customers, though. You've identified your customer. Take care of them. You've identified those who will never be your customer. Don't worry about them and don't advertise your art in the wrong places. This almost goes without saying. I'd argue that you should only mix controversial subjects in with your brand personality if they're an integral part of your branding; then make sure you're pretty good at deflecting arrows.

7. Fairs, exhibitions, pop-up shops and other events

There is something of a disagreement between myself and my daughter about what should come first - online or direct sales. It may be that the older crafters among us are more likely to lean towards craft fairs. The younger group are more likely to start online. Kira argues that starting off selling online is a great way to quickly test your product against the global market, and identify where your customers might be, without investing too much time and money. My plea, however, is that fairs are the most fun you can have while running a craft business and so should come first ...in life, and in the book. And fairs are where you get to decide if your business can help fund your love of travel.

Hobby fairs and exhibitions are a great way to connect with the public, flex your marketing, and test whether there's any interest at all in your work, though do bear in mind you may not always encounter your ideal audience. You may be tempted to under-price here to test the water - don't. Be prepared to lose sales the first few times out and simply connect with the public and talk to them. Get a feel for the market. See what other people do, and accept feedback. Don't accept only positive feedback, or get hung up on the negative. Weigh them both up and act on these comments. Don't ever be put off by the customer who says "Pah! That's too expensive, I could make it myself!". There is always one of these. Funnily enough, the higher up your tree you climb, and the higher your prices, the fewer of these you meet. Lose that customer and be happy to do so. Smile and try to get a genuine "excellent...enjoy your crafting" out from between your gritted teeth. If she can and does make it herself, she will have a new respect for your pricing… or possibly not. You shouldn't take an ounce of notice of this one either way.

Preparing for a fair and making your stand attractive

Failing to prepare is preparing to fail. This is so true when attending fairs. I've had fairs where my lack of preparedness has affected my stand, which has affected my mood and confidence and, in turn, this has affected my sales. For the small things, however, there is always another friendly stand holder who will need your pins or will lend you his scissors!

For most events, if you can afford any extra costs you might incur, you will be more comfortable taking someone with you who can take over when you need a break and something to eat, like a partner or good friend. Don't spend the whole time chatting to each other though, and be sure to try and engage with all the passersby where possible.

Having done miniatures fairs for 30 years (good grief!), these are my thoughts on what you might need to pack and consider for a fair. Some of the items are more specific to small items like miniatures or jewellery, for some you may need to consider how to display various items of clothing or other, more complicated products. Consider how your items need to be displayed. My packing has always been heavier on the display items and lighter on the stock because I'm a miniaturist and I travel by air. In some cases, it may be in your interests to make a list of items to purchase at your destination when doing international events. This could include heavy items such as extension cables, disposable cloths and even lighting.

Table covers: you'll need large pieces of fabric sufficient not only for the length of the table but also to drop down the front and sides. If the back of the stand is visible while walking round the hall (i.e. if your stand is part of an "island"), you may need to cover the back too. If you have a wall stand it's easier to leave it open for storage of bags boxes and extra stock. You need overnight covers too for weekend or week-long fairs or if you're alone and need to nip to the loo. I use organdie because it's very light weight and strong, translucent and very pretty. Think about the way you display your products. What will your background colour be? Make sure your table colour and its texture don't take your customers eye before your work does, and that it will show your work off in its best light possible.

Display materials for your point of sale (POS): merchandising stands, display boards, signage and more. If you're travelling by air or public transport the weight of these is extremely important. Every gram less of display material is a gram more of saleable stock you can take. If your stock is small and expensive and reasonably light weight you can spend more of your weight allowance on better quality POS materials but, for most of us, carrying the most stock possible is important. Make sure when coming up with design ideas that your display materials don't distract from your work. For example, I have a miniaturist friend who hit upon the idea of both carry-ing and displaying her beautiful materials in small pretty card suitcases. It sounds like a great idea. Packing in and displaying on the same little cases. The display was certainly attractive. But she wasn't selling anything. The problem was easy to see. The pretty suitcase display was the star of the stand and, although it was artistic, it drew the eye and the mind away from the miniatures displayed on and within them. Her display would have been perfect had she been selling socks or underwear spilling out of the suitcases or had she picked simpler, less pretty ones. Spend some time at home building a stand at the size, or the various sizes, that will be available at the venue. And be self-critical. Or ask a friend or partner and listen to their concerns. Don't ask a lovely friend who always says what you want to hear. Ask a critical one. They are your real best friends in business. Do develop confidence in your own style. This will help you to get used to the materials you'll need. Remember, not all tables have the same style, and some will be suitable for clamps and some not.

Clamps: these can be very useful when mounting a stand, gripping table covers, and for security, but look at several different styles of tabletop. You may need wooden blocks to back thin tables with deep edges, for example. Our items are really small and so we find some kind of 'terraced' stand is a good idea. But we normally travel by air, so our stand has to be extremely lightweight and easy to mount. We have a collapsible semicircle stand for the centre of our stand. It's hand cut out of foam core board and we can spray paint and/or fabric cover it or remake this when it gets really tatty.

Lighting: good lighting is really important at a fair, as you can't guarantee that the lighting in the venue will be any good. Practise with the lights you've bought and see if they really are suitable for your work. Clip-on lights are often best and usually LED. There are a couple of different colour lights for LED; there's the standard cool white and a warmer colour. Generally, the whiter colour is better for exhibitions. But the bluer spectrum is cold

and may not be the same colour that you did your work under. This can cause real problems. It's often best to choose similar lighting to work under as you will use for your display. If colour is a big part of your work, you may be terribly disappointed in how your work appears under your display lighting. Your work may look fabulous in daylight or in a warm light, but nobody will know that if they don't buy the work they can see under your lighting (for polymer clay artists, I write more about the knotty subject of metamerism in my Colour Book). If you have any lights or anything else that needs plugging in, don't forget a lightweight extension lead.

Display height: think about raising the height of your work to nearer eye level, especially if your items are small and difficult to see. Customers will spend more time looking at your display if it's comfortable to do so because bending over low tables can give you what we call 'exhibition-neck'. You have to learn to be a bit of a DIYer and sometimes make quick-fix decisions if you arrive at a fair and the shape and size and height of the table isn't what you expect. Make sure you have items on hand to do this with. Folding plate racks, for example, can raise a stand with the use of cable ties and gaffer tape.

Sticky hands: for our miniatures, we have a trick to keep little children's sticky hands off our work and that is having two magnifiers on our stand. These are very useful for elderly collectors but an irresistible draw for children. Just holding the spy glass keeps their sticky hands busy. Have two or even three, and 'fiddle fingers' will be a problem of the past. I advise you to keep a bag of treats (seconds of your work or ribbons or craft materials are good), for the children who pick the spy glasses up and admire your work rather than touching it. I have customers now who were those children 10 or 20 years ago. A creative child never forgets an unexpected gift of something cute or shiny.

Other kinds of sticky fingers: There are people who specialise in stealing at fairs. Some taking the stock and some looking to swipe the takings. So far, we have never fallen victim to the latter and if we've had the former it has been so light that we haven't noticed. This is largely because our most valuable things are further back on the stand. But we are pretty vigilant and have plenty of experience of the signs that someone may be considering "accidentally" not paying for an item. We have small trays for selection of loose items because those things are of low value individually but, once in the tray, they are difficult to disappear with. You only need to keep half an eye on the tray and not intimidate your lovely honest customers. There is the act of "showing a friend an item". In this trick, something disappears behind the back of another customer. Because that's a red flag, we simply visibly up our vigilance. Anyone with intent can see that we aren't an easy target and will usually move on.

Despite this, don't imagine that every customer whose behaviour is a little odd is dishonest. Most of them are just ordinary people with unusual behaviour patterns. How wrong you can be sometimes! Once, I thought a customer must be attempting to take something because of the way she turned my items over and over. She looked around at me, and then went back to the behaviour. It turned out she simply didn't understand how I could put such fine detailing right through my pieces! Once she understood after about half an hour of screwing up her face over a few pieces, several went into her tray and she has become one of my very best customers. And a lovely lady she is too! So be open minded. Customers are 98.5% joy, 1% confusion and less than 1% trouble.

Mindset at a fair

You simply have to try your best to be engaging at events like these, whether it comes naturally to you or not. Try to imagine you're the star of your very own show. Pay attention to your appearance but also to your mood. I've had bad fairs simply because my heart wasn't in it. This is usually because I felt underprepared or because I arrived late with very little time to make the best job of my display and pricing. If you're anxious or stressed, you can look awkward behind your stand. This can be difficult as many creatives lean towards being introverts, and I myself am one of these. However, if you ask a cross section of my customers if I'm an introvert or an extrovert they would say the latter. I've simply learned to perform. That doesn't mean that my warmth towards visitors to my stand is any less genuine, it's just that my social anxiety is now under control, largely because I've done it so often. It's not unusual to have these anxieties, and you simply have to "fake it 'til you make it". You'll soon find that you become comfortable in these situations. You learn to save your anxiety for the preparation time, and the exhaustion until the end of the day.

Making the most of fairs

"How do I get people to look at my stand?"

My stand is often one of the busiest at the miniatures fairs. Much to the annoyance of my neighbours. This is because I've decided on the correct current positioning and merchandising of my business (after I had set the business up badly in the first place).

The collectors who pass by my stand at fairs see some of the best mid-price work available. In an earlier chapter I explained why I got stuck at this price level. Now I will tell you why I now find that it suits me. When I first became a miniaturist, I'd hit upon some ideas which hadn't been fully explored by the miniatures world at the time. I pretty quickly identified that my place in this world was as a sharer of ideas and not a guarder of secrets. I also found that sharing was, in my case, also selling. So, my customers are pretty much everyone who is interested in miniatures whether they collect or make, or both.

In order to make the best of the opportunities presented for you at a fair, you have the option of waiting for that one customer who will pay a small fortune for something really special, and take the risk that they won't appear. Or, you need to attempt to make sure every customer who passes your stand sees something that they may want to buy. You need to think in tiers. This isn't difficult because many merchandising display stands are made with tiered steps. Even if yours aren't, you need to have a focal point. Customers at fairs are divided into categories. You want every category to stop at your stand. Making your stand attractive, however, is another issue. For now, we'll look at your stock balance.

I have something for each type of miniatures customer. The first type is the wealthy collector who is looking for a smaller something they haven't seen before. As I say, my work is mid-priced, but it is innovative. I'm often first to the market with a new technique. This collector would pay more if I had higher priced items and displayed them in a different way, but my allowance of time and focus means my balance cannot be exclusively towards them. The next is the less-wealthy collector. I lean towards these customers' needs because my style of work, by the nature of the fact that I teach, won't stay exclusive for long. They know that they are getting work from a "name", but at an affordable price. Because of that price level, I also attract the trader, but I don't tend to offer trade discounts (wholesale prices) at fairs, except perhaps in the last hour or two of the fair. Now we come to crafters. For them, I have kits and moulds and stencils and, as most of my customers know, usually a demonstration. They are open to new ideas and willing to spend a little money on something which is going to add to their inspiration. Then finally, there are my major and (shh, don't tell anyone) my favourite customers: the maker-traders. They are interesting, excitable and, well, very much like me! They will buy from me where I can help them have more fun and make more profit. They want to know what I can do for them this time. Over the years I've met and encouraged a lot of younger miniaturists, just as I was encouraged myself. Some are clearly destined to be exclusive and keepers of secrets. Some will be teachers and sharers. Ask yourself which of these groups do you want to be your major customers, but don't forget that you can appeal to more than one group. In my opinion you can never mix absolute top price OOAK exclusivity with realistic sales of tools and tips for makers, because work you teach won't stay exclusive for long. In either market you can make a living. Making a good living is another matter.

Obviously, many of you reading this won't be miniaturists, and your customer types may be different, but the principle of finding who you want to appeal to and at what level remains the same.

I mentioned demonstrating at fairs. I have always demonstrated. I've found that if you demonstrate or even just make some of your work between chats to customers, your stand will be a magnet. The event organisers will notice that too. And event organisers know that if you are winning customers by keeping them entertained, they win visitors because people are coming in greater numbers. Most fair organisers know that It's a win-win strategy for them to offer those stand holders who demonstrate extra space for free. This is a bit of a secret so, shhh, don't say I told you! But it makes sense. Ask yourself, out of two events, which would you be most likely to go to: the stuffy navel gazing one, or the one where there's some inspiration to be had? It's also a much more effective sales technique than free sweets or pretty business cards, though these are useful too! And, this way, you get to know your customers, and they come back over and over. If, in addition, you're selling craft kits for the hobby end of the market, you have a sure-fire winner. For me, as a slight introvert behind an extrovert exterior, demonstrating also brings me out of myself. I don't do cold selling, but I do hot selling. I love what I do, and the enthusiasm shows...and sells.

> *Takeaway*: If you're well prepared for a fair both in the physical display and in your mental preparation, you will have a more successful fair. Some fairs fall flat because of poor organisation. If YOU are ready you will get the best possible results out of every event. If you're the one interesting (and interested) stand holder, you can still make a success out of a badly-run event by exciting every member of the public who comes through the door. They may not even buy at that event. But they will remember you and talk about you.

Travel: The best thing about being a craftsperson

I've made no secret of the fact that craftspeople in general don't often get rich. Quite the opposite. Apart from immersing myself into the wonderful world of creativity, having my crafts materials paid for, not having to get up if I don't want to, and working whichever days of the week I want to (usually all of them), what has being a miniaturist ever done for me? It has to be international travel. I'm sure that's the part that most 9-5 working people are quietly envious of, too.

You even get to choose where to go and when. How to travel and where to stay and the business pays for it all. That is, as long as it's 'cattle class' and in the cheaper quarter of the city, often buying eggs in the supermarket and boiling them up for breakfast in your own portable kettle, against the rules of the hotel. Yes, you can go anywhere, and I have. If you have more success of course, you can ramp up the class and quality of hotels and transport. But, by keeping to frugal travelling principles, I've been to Australia, Japan, New York and Philadelphia. I've been invited (but unable to go) to Indonesia and China, and I've done fairs or classes or both in almost every country in Europe. And it's been a lot of fun. Seeing the sights, trying the food, the languages, getting to know the people and of course meeting up with some of the best miniaturists in the world. And finding they are all "just like us". You need to make sure it pays you to travel, or covers its costs, or at the very least that it's somewhere that you really want to go. So much so that you're even prepared to take a bit of a loss. The deeper into being a crafter as your full-time profession you get, the less of a loss you can take, and the more you have to seek out cost savings. But if you follow my advice about keeping all your receipts and about choosing the right events for you (coming up) you can, in theory, travel the world. And where most people have to pay the full cost of their travel, in theory, the taxman part pays for yours!

Of course, the reality is that it has to pay its way; you have to pay rent or mortgage and utilities and eat just like anyone else, and that can be a struggle on a very limited income. One of the reasons I've managed to get away with it is because I teach my craft. If teaching a class for one or two days covers your travel and hotel costs, then the fair just has to take care of itself. And if you make those the costs of the trip when you are just a side hustle it's working for expenses.

Teaching workshops means you are a bit more stressed in advance of a trip, have more weight to carry and have to spend more time away from home. The upside is that being able to teach can be a very valuable skill and pay for those trips. This rather makes up for the fact that when you teach a dozen people some of them are going to come into the business and are going to compete for the same customers. Swings and round-abouts. But they're paying for that privilege, often twice because they will also be your best customers at the fair. You have sold them on your wonderful techniques and now they want the tools, the materials, the books and some examples to aim for. An added bonus is that many of them are also going to turn into some of your best friends!

Often the organisers will ask you to provisionally book their fairs six months or longer in advance. This can be quite an outlay. You really have to be certain that you want to go to the place before saying yes. If you're thinking of travelling with cheaper airline operators, it can pay you to book the flights without any luggage. This way you can fix it at a very cheap rate well in advance and take the possible loss if you have to cancel the trip. This would happen if the class is under subscribed or the fair is cancelled. You then only add the extras when your class is full, and the fair is confirmed.

To help you decide whether you're going for business or just for fun, or if at all, it's worth preparing a spread-sheet of craft fairs. Include all the costs and the potential income. One thing that's undeniable, foreign fairs can be lots of fun. Anywhere you haven't been before should be on your list, even if only as a visitor. Fairs in different countries can open you up to a new audience, and you can see a different side to the hobby. In some places it's highly developed. In some places over-developed and can feel tired. Maybe, if you have something new to offer, this is just what they are waiting for. In some countries you can feel the youth and burgeoning enthusiasm. Some peoples defy their stereotypes, and some confirm them; but one thing you must do is take a few extra days really to find that out for yourself, and to broaden your own mind.

> *Travel hacks:* Travel with your most valuable stock in your hand luggage and your clothes and toiletries in your main luggage. Minimise your clothing, take non-crushable items. Lightweight and layering clothes, merino wool socks, vest and jumper (as merino is moisture-wicking, it can be worn for a long time without getting a sweaty smell). Keep to the "one on, one spare" principle. Consider a collapsible travel kettle. Think weight, weight, weight. Get the biggest allowable 4-wheeled suitcase if your stock is heavy, you can pad out with a fibre pillow. If it's light, you can get a lot more in a very big case.

Choosing your fairs

Choosing which fairs to go to isn't easy because, unless your fair is very close, it's going to cost you a lot! You need to take into account all the obvious costs. The table, the travel, the accommodation. The lost work time, the replacement of the stock you've just sold at a lower profit simply because your selling costs are higher. Many crafters and artists, when they start out, just want to be seen. And, of course, we all need to be seen to raise our profile and connect with our customers but, since the cost can often outweigh the income, we have to choose our fairs more carefully.

Making careful calculations on costs can help you sway the decision. Remember, travel is not just business but it has to help your business and your creativity in some way. To what extent can you afford a poor fair for the pleasure of attending in a lovely city?

Keep these costs in mind:

- *Return air fares or train fares (for two people?)*
- *Airport or railway parking and petrol to get there, plus mileage and any wear-and-tear on the car*
- *Lost days of work preparing travelling and attending the fair, sometimes for two of you*
- *Table cost*
- *Accommodation*

- *Meals*
- *Cost of production of your sold stock in time and materials*

This would be an expensive fair to go to and simply look at and extra nights will cost you extra accommodation and meals. If you made a loss and you didn't enjoy the experience you will be left feeling that you could have kept your outlay in the bank, sold online, and just taken a holiday on the difference.

So, what would make you want to do a fair? Let me give you another scenario. This same size of fair now costs you less because you squeeze every cost. In terms of air fares, only one of you travels so the airfares are halved, no airport parking but your partner has to do double the driving and wear-and-tear on the car. The table costs are the same, but the fair organiser gave you a discount because she likes you and wants to bring you to her fair. You might decide that this was more profitable, but less enjoyable. These days I don't tend to think of fairs as very profitable in themselves. They used to be. But they're important to my plan to meet and greet my customers from time to time.

Takeaway: Fairs can be the most exciting part of your year. Not only that but the travel can be like a free holiday paid for on the business several times a year. If travelling is your very favourite thing, do the maths. If it's not a loss, it's a life profit.

Wholesale

At any time in your business life, an interested person can come to you for wholesale terms. Be ready for this, as it can happen in-person at events, and you want to be prepared. Always have a margin you can cut if you want big orders. Ask yourself what the economies of scale are for you, and whether it's actually possible or desirable to sell wholesale. If you don't want to sell wholesale, don't be afraid to say no. A really eager customer will pay your full price. Others will go somewhere else if you refuse.

But don't be afraid to stick to your guns if someone comes to you with a ridiculously low offer. I was approached by a company once in the beginning of the nail art fad for my fruit slices as sliceable canes. The gentleman insisted that I must discount further and, for-

tunately, I was a bit annoyed by his insistent tone and said no I mustn't. If I had realised just how big the customer was intending these orders to be, I might have been overawed and swayed, but I didn't, and so I put my foot down. Later that day I got an order for two thousand pounds' worth of canes for him, and later for another four. Six thousand pounds' worth of orders for my little craft item in one day.

Over the next year I had several orders of this size. My problem then was keeping up with demand. This, of course, was a problem in itself. It can cause problems with cash flow buying materials. My material costs were significant, but payment for orders was swift and before postage, so for me this wasn't too difficult. I had the choice then of becoming an employer, but I really wasn't big enough to take on someone whose payroll I would then have to administer, so I chose to subcontract. We had a really good year before the far east companies copied everything. Bubbles happen, and they burst. Don't pin everything on huge wholesale orders from one or two companies, as they can just as soon stop ordering.

Galleries

Wow, a gallery is interested in your work! They will double your prices, of course, but this shouldn't worry or panic you. If they think they can double, they must think that at least some of your work is worth it. They double your prices because they believe they can make that much profit. Don't let anyone display your work on a sale or return basis, unless you are prepared to lose it. They deserve to sell your lovely product only if they are prepared for the outlay. You can and should set your wholesale prices for them in order to make a sale and for the prestige of being in that shop or gallery.

Most companies these days want your work at half the price. Selling wholesale does take most of the postage and packing admin and keeping customers happy away, which may be worth that half. But be prepared for burnout. More on coping with stress and burnout later in the book.

Takeaway: Offer small discounts (perhaps 25-30%) for smaller orders or non-prestigious companies. Offer larger discounts for prestigious galleries and locations, or for larger orders which take the huge admin job off your shoulders, or for products which are easier to reproduce.

8. Product photography for beginners

"How do people get those nice smart photographs which seem to jump off the screen?"

So now we have our plan, we have our price. We have a few products and we may even have done a little craft fair. What is the next logical step? Well, it always comes back to marketing, of course, but first we need some gorgeous images!

The major thing which will set your work apart from the competition, apart from its quality, is the quality and "pop" of your images. Your photographs don't have to be

in transparent background illustrations, over or under text, or within cut-out text.

Although I think of myself as an amateur photographer, my experience is with photographing the production of miniatures step-by-step for publication. When the work you do means that each step will destroy the last, you can't go back and simply do it again, so it's very important to get each step right. The following are my "hacks" to getting professional-looking photographs with an amateur set-up.

Firstly, you need a camera that's up to the job. That may well be your smartphone these days, especially if

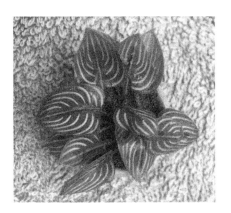  

professionally taken, but they should look as if they have been, and in many cases this is possible simply with your smartphone. Your image has to jump off the screen and make your potential customer want to look again and much closer. If they do, you're halfway to a sale. If two businesses sell identical products, the one with the more attractive photographs is more likely to get higher sales. Above are three pictures of a miniature potted plant.

One on a really bad background both in terms of colour and texture. Avoid both, unless you absolutely do need a background or if your item is bright white. One is in bad light. You can salvage it and bring up the colour, but it's hard work and will be a bit patchy and the colours will be blotchy. One has been taken in good light on a white background. This is sharp enough to use in publications or on websites and social media. You can cut it out to use as a design element in a programme like Photoshop, Canva or similar, and you'll be able to use it

you're adept at adjusting the brightness settings on your phone camera. If you're buying a smartphone to use as a camera, either for video or stills, look for the camera capability. For small items such as jewellery, art pieces and miniatures, if you can afford to, get a camera or phone with a macro lens or macro capability and a timer. Having said that, we are currently just using a smartphone, and having decent results. If you want to produce photographs which are printable on merchandise, you need a good digital SLR camera, however that's not my area of experience.

Image Resolution

I hope you aren't afraid of creepy-crawlies.

I admit I had to ask my husband to explain image resolution to me, so now I'll try to break it down for you. Here are 2 images in 2 different resolutions. This little

image at 300dpi

image at 60dpi

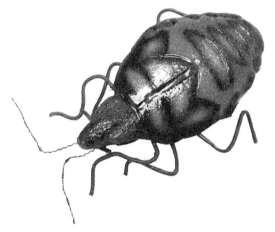

bug was only about 2.5cm long in real life. Here's why it's important that you use no less than 200 dpi (dots per inch). Now we can talk about pixels and centimetres. It's best you know what both mean so that photographers or printing departments or websites like Redbubble don't bamboozle you. Oh no, maths! Simply put, and rounded up a bit, if you have an image which is 100 pixels wide, it's not going to look really sharp if it's printed more than a centimetre wide. Here he is at just 60 dpi and here at 300dpi (the best we had at the time the photograph was taken).

When both are printed as a small image, you can't really tell the difference. Now when I try to size it up this is what we get. So, the tiny bug looks OK tiny at both 60dpi and 300dpi, but look how awful the low resolution is when sized up to 5cm whereas the 300dpi one looks just fine. This is why printing companies like Redbubble insist on a certain minimum resolution. The better your resolution, the larger they can print your image without it looking grainy or pixelated. Even though my little bug was a reasonable resolution for publication in my colour book, it is a bit small for Redbubble. Redbubble is mentioned in the multiple income streams chapter. If you are working with Redbubble, you can take a relatively small image like this one and multiply it either at home or in their software. Their tools only give you a limited set of options on multiplying your image.

The higher quality you can get, the better. 300 dpi is preferable, and you should ideally never go below 150 dpi. Generally, to get anything much better than this you are looking at professional level and that means expensive.

Bear in mind that there's nothing wrong with buying second-hand equipment, including cameras and phones, just ensure that the lens isn't scratched before you buy.

We currently use my iPhone 6s or a 41megapixel Nokia. Although it's a phone, it was bought to be used as a camera. Because of its excellent lens we use it for both stills and videos. Make or buy a tripod or stand to hold your camera. Ours is a bodge-job with wood and elastic bands but you don't see that from the photos, so who cares?

The very most important 3 considerations are light, light and…light!

We're lucky that we live in Andalusia where usually there's plenty of sun. But don't take pictures in full sun even if you have it. It has to be diffused to avoid heavy shadows. So, our lightwell is a lucky part of self-building. It's a white room with a glass roof. If you live in a place with less sun, I recommend a conservatory if you have one and get some white sheets or some fleece that will let light in but diffuse it a little and bounce it around the room. You won't always be able to photograph in diffused daylight. If you can, then you should augment this with extra lights.

If photographing small items, you can build yourself a large white-walled box to sit on your table. This is to bounce the light backwards and forwards all over your work so that as much light falls on it as possible, from as many directions as possible. This is in order to reduce shadows. If your room is painted in dark colours, this is even more important. Or get a wheeled trolley and build a white walled box to sit on it. Then, on every corner of your box, put a lamp aimed toward the middle and, above your head, put as big a bulb in your lamp as you can. Or even have an array of several lamps. You can choose to put several colours of bulb in it to make sure you have the biggest possible spectrum of colour (this is a whole subject covered for polymer clay in my Colour Book). We switch ours on when the day is dull or to extend my work hours if the sun is just rising or setting. But I would avoid photographing in the hours of darkness if at all possible.

I also have a 'toy' which I designed and a friend of mine made, which I've never used since we came here. It's basically a DIY ring light, just a box with a circular fluorescent light on an adjustable pole above it. These days you can buy very reasonably priced LED ring lights which have become very popular for vloggers and make up artists for evenly lighting faces (Kira's cost £32 on Amazon, it has 3 settings and fully adjustable height). I also use mine for live classes in my workshop. These can also be used as overhead lights for macro photography, and can also function as a tripod for your camera even when you're not using the light. Do bear in mind that some ring lights are designed to only hold a phone, and some are only designed to hold a standard camera, although some do both. Another option is to go to a photography shop, if you have any disposable capital, and buy a photographer's light tent. We've never invested money in that but, so far, we haven't needed to.

Photograph against a white background in almost every case. You can change your background colour later if you must but currently people prefer white and also it helps you to clean up any colour problems. You don't need an expensive set up for this either. I know a number of crafters who shoot their photographs on top of cheap white Ikea coffee tables, or white goods such as tumble driers. Anything with a clean, matte, pure white surface can do, to start out with!

Don't try anything too complex, like photographing on graded backgrounds. All of that stuff can be done post-photography too, and it's all been done a thousand times before anyway. Just get a big white piece of paper, curl it up against the back wall to create a curved backdrop and put your work on it. The curve helps to create a lack of angles, reducing the appearance of shadows and helping to create a clean background. With your item positioned against the white backdrop, set your camera to macro (if you have it) and/or touch the screen of your smartphone until you have a nice sharp focus. If it simply won't focus close up, you will have to take the picture from a little further away. When all is good to go, click! Is there a more attractive angle? Try it! Do you want your hands in the shot? Set it to timer then go! If you're photographing processes for a tutorial, check that you have some good photos coming out, then just go for it, taking several different shots of each stage. Expect to take a huge number of photos at each angle. Spend some time finding the best ones at the end.

One little trick I do when photographing my own hands is to place a business card or calling card (ideally with small writing) at the depth where my hands will be. I click to focus on the card, set the timer, and then remove the card, placing my hands back in shot. It usually works! This is also good for ultra-close ups where there are still things at several depths. The business card will set the highest of the depths and anything behind will still look good. If you try to focus on a deeper part, you can lose the higher parts.

So now you have the best, sharpest image possible to work with, and you can then use all the tools on your photo editing software to make it even better. This is pretty simple if your background is clean and white because any colour balance issues will be easily rectified by setting the white back to a 'proper' paper white. For example, if your image comes out too blue or too yellow, one simple adjustment back to a plain white background can solve a lot of basic problems.

If photographing larger items, such as clothing or large artworks, you may need to back your lighting off a long way. Have as many sources as possible from as many different directions and remember to light your model from underneath as well as above. Shadows from overhead lighting may be moody but are unlikely to make your work or your model look their best. There may be times to use unusual lighting, such as at Halloween, however, your goal is usually to just have a sharp and well-lit image, without harsh shadows.

Whatever size you're working with, remember the spectrum of the light you're working with will affect your basic picture, but you can usually tweak that later in Photoshop, GIMP, or whatever photo editing software you're using. The key is to get enough light and good focus.

One thing is for certain. If you get a really good image, under really good diffused light and on a white background, anyone who knows anything about images (for example a magazine's art department) will know what to do to present your work at its very best. If you're completely stuck, there are people on websites like Fiverr who can do a batch for you for...well, around a fiver each, more or less. If you are photographing rooms remember the lighting and the timing and put your calling card in the middle (or a bit further forward) of the scene, and experiment to find which depth gives you the best focus

When you have your first lovely pictures, keep your very best in a file you call something like "best images", so you know where to go for all your most beautiful shots. If you can learn the photo editing skills, get into the habit of making compilations of these for promotions. When you need to get your hands on something quickly for an interview or poster opportunity, they'll be easily available and save you hours of serious last-minute stress and possible mess-ups and lost opportunities.

Photo editing

If you can get a nice well-lit picture with a bright white background, then this is generally best practice. If this is tricky for you to achieve, you do have the option of cutting out the image and placing it onto a white background using software like GIMP or Photoshop. GIMP (GNU Image Manipulation Programme) is a photo editing programme you can download for free, with many of the same capabilities as Photoshop. If you have a high budget, Photoshop is great, but most people don't need it for small craft item photography. On these programs you can even add a "drop shadow" to add a slightly more realistic definition. This can take a long time, especially with products that have a complex shape. If you have a large batch of images you want to be cut out, you can outsource this work to someone cheaply using a website for freelancers such as Fiverr. You can also use these options to add watermarks to your images, if you choose. This can help to prevent copyists from using your images without permission to promote their own work which, sadly, does happen.

Sometimes, even if your picture is well lit with no heavy shadows, the colour just doesn't look true to life on the image or doesn't quite "pop" enough. Perhaps you're even gone overboard with the lighting, which could make it look washed-out, or you're using the wrong light setting. If the light settings or bulbs are too "cold", your images can have a blue hue. Conversely, if your lighting is too "warm", your images can take on orange tones. In this case it can help to experiment with the brightness and contrast settings of your image before using them. This ensures they look as bright and attractive as your products do in person.

When you're uploading pictures to Instagram, you have the option of adding filters to your image, designed to help you improve your photo, as well as being able to adjust things like brightness and contrast within the app. You can click through the filters to see all the available effects. These can be fun, particularly for personal images, but be careful when using these with product photography, as they can change the colouring and tones of the image. You don't want a customer to complain that an item they bought doesn't look the same as the photos. You can enhance your images, but make sure that any product images stay as true to life as possible.

When you're using images online, you want them to be as high-quality as they can be. However, if the file size of the image is too large, then this can cause your web pages to take a long time to load. This is off putting for most web users. To reduce this effect, there are websites that will reduce your image file sizes for you (for free), while maintaining the image quality. Our favourite is www.tinypng.com - with this, you simply upload your images, the website compresses the file size for you, and you download them again to be used on your website. Always keep the original, largest file size "master copy" of your images for future use, though. Put all of the images you have reduced the file size of or edited into a new folder named "optimised" or "edited" or similar.

Takeaway: Good images are crucial to your marketing and so it's well worth your while investing time or even money in learning more. With practise you can certainly get good quality images from a good smartphone these days. Think light, light and more light and try to photograph on a white background. The rest can be done afterwards, by someone else if necessary.

9. Start selling online

"Do I need a website?"

If you are new to the business and are a bit perplexed about the whole digital world, especially if you aren't a 'young thing' and you're worried that you may not be able to make it without a website, there are ways of selling which completely avoid the need for one. Well, here I have to admit, I haven't made all the mistakes. At least not on my own. Lucky for me, I married a 'computer geek' who has always helped me with everything computer and internet related.

If you don't have a website, do you really need one? Even though I do have one and most of our trade comes through it, I do think it is possible to build a small one person craft business these days without one. But you have to realise that it will always be very small unless you have a strong online presence. Increasingly, shoppers prefer to buy online and, even if they prefer to purchase in a physical setting, many will research brands and options online first. Even if you think that your target market prefers not to shop online (such as some older customers). It is wise to cover all bases, and appealing to the younger generation can help with the longevity of your business. Most businesses have an online presence these days, and this helps in building "brand authority", ensuring that your company is seen as a strong contender in the market.

One good reason to have a website is as a management system. Make sure you know the difference between a simple website without e-commerce (sales) facilities, and one with a back-end management system. Be careful you ask for and get what you want. Don't pay a lot for the former. The latter is more complicated and you would need some investment. But, let's face it, unless you have the ability to write code (programming language), this type of website is one you should be prepared to pay for. But watch out for sophisticated sales techniques for ultimately disappointing results. Not many really good code writers are really slick salespeople. And vice versa. You have been warned.

Building your own website VS outsourcing

"Should I build my own site?"

You have to look very carefully at an investment in time and money for having your own site against letting someone else do the work for a small cut, whether that is hiring a web developer, or using a pre-existing online marketplace (more on these later on). I certainly think if I didn't have a computer-savvy partner who was as creative as me and equally unlikely to fit himself into a 9-5 job, well, honestly, I may not bother. The fact that he does all this work pays for itself in increased sales but to be honest, not much more than that. Fortunately, there are other business-related things my computer geek husband does for me that are worth even more. Some of these things I could do for myself, like photographic optimisation, and some I would struggle with, such as video and publishing work. I may have bothered with an off-the-peg website builder as a sole trader in the past. Ultimately, however, one person simply cannot be all things at all times and it's often better to sell through other media who do all the IT work for you and take a commission.

So, if you don't have a website, you need to be looking at other outlets for online selling, such as Etsy, eBay and even Amazon. There are also online craft fairs which are worth trying. You won't make a lot of income from any of these individually, but if you use them all the trickle is more likely to become a stream. You will find which of these work for you. Some you have to pay a monthly fee rather than or in addition to a transaction fee, and so you'll need to close channels that don't sell your type of work well. As I have always had the benefit of my own tame coder, that's about as far as I can go on the subject of online platforms. So I'm going to hand over to Kira who has a start-up's experience on how most new businesses are using the platforms which cope with all the back-end issues (at a cost per sale or per month).

Where can I sell online?

Unless you are, or know, a skilled web developer with a flair for coding, you will want an easy way to sell your goods over the internet, at least in your first years. There are two main types of eCommerce (online retail) platform you can use to sell your handmade items: via online marketplaces (such as Etsy or eBay), or by creating your own individual website using an online website builder.

For the broadest reach, I recommend using both channels (known as omni-channel retailing), since multiple revenue streams are always a good thing. However, this isn't always necessary. Many new businesses will find that the costs of maintaining your own eCommerce website can outweigh the income generated, and therefore a platform such as Etsy can often be the highest earner, with the lowest work required. This makes it a good place to gauge the market and analyse your competition.

In this chapter we will outline the functions, costs and benefits of each of these, giving you some of the core

Marketplace Platforms Pros and Cons

Marketplace & Fees	Pros	Cons
Etsy Listing fees ($0.20 USD per item), transaction fees (5% of your item and delivery prices). Etsy Ads Fees (optional), Offsite Ads fees (not optional). Option for $10 monthly subscription fee to "Etsy Plus".	Largest global online marketplace for craftspeople = broader reach, high global SERP ranking. Wide product range with 160 categories, including clothes, tools and adult items, where some other site ranges are narrower. Their new offsite ads feature effectively runs paid ads for you which may be useful for some vendors. Etsy remains a great place to start out and test your products for the market before investing in a more costly eCommerce website.	With quite a saturated market, you must use good SEO and outside promotion to drive sales. Etsy recently introduced "offsite ads", which means some sellers incur additional costs if an item is sold via one of these ads, whether they like it or not. This can boost sales, but it can also be costly, charging 15% of the total sale amount when an item is bought. If you made less than 10,000 USD on Etsy in the past 365 days, you can opt out of Offsite Ads, although you are automatically enrolled. For anyone earning over that amount in a year, Offsite Ads is not optional, so this could potentially result in sellers losing a very large chunk of income against their will.
eBay Standard listing fee + final value fee for each item. You can subscribe to eBay Shop packages which offer a storefront with customisable features and listing credits. Prices for these start at £25 per month.	Wider product range than Etsy, but with more niche categories than Amazon, which attract a different audience (including antiques and collectables). Like Amazon, this site does tend to attract the "bargain-hunter" type of shopper, rather than the crowd who appreciate handmade detail. This is ideal if you have a large amount of craft supplies to sell, but less ideal for your actual art.	Larger mass market websites such as Etsy and Amazon give you less of an opportunity to express your business personality, and provide less customer loyalty than the sites with a focus on handmade products. Additionally, selling on sites like eBay and Etsy allows for less branding and individuality than having your own website might, making it harder to stand out against your competitors. Also, it may be harder to get press attention with an eBay or Etsy store than it would be with your own branded website.
Amazon Low-volume sales incur a fee of £0.75 per item (plus additional fees in some cases), but if you make over 35 sales per month you can subscribe to a "Pro" seller account for £25 per month.	Household name, already used by millions of online shoppers. It does feature the "Fulfilled by Amazon" shipping option which is useful for some sellers.	As it is such a large mass-market platform, it is harder for small handmade art businesses to be seen on Amazon. As such, it attracts a slightly different audience, too. The cost to list products on Amazon can potentially be a little higher than on eBay.

Handmade at Amazon	Sellers must submit an application to be considered eligible. This does provide a certain feel of exclusivity, and ensures your work will not be sold alongside mass-produced items. Also, listings don't expire, meaning you don't need to remember to renew them.	Amazon only pays out funds from your sales once every two weeks, unlike Etsy which usually dispatches funds within 48 hours of a sale. Due to the application process, apparently it could take weeks or even months to be approved and start selling. Also, there are only 14 product categories to choose from.
This can reportedly be quite expensive in fees. Though there is no listing fee, there is a per-item referral fee of 12-15% of the sale value, which will be changing to a flat rate of 15% as of December 31, 2021.		
Folksy	Smaller than Etsy, but the largest UK based online marketplace for craftspeople, meaning it's a less saturated market. Cute, almost twee style, great for selling products such as jewellery, homeware, teddy bears and greetings cards.	This has a narrower product range than Etsy does, with a sort of twee and cutesy handmade feel. Great if you're making twee or cutesy products, but possibly a less useful platform for artists who are making more adult or "edgy" work.
£0.15 + VAT for each item listed, 6% + VAT sales commission on the selling price of all items. Option for £5 monthly subscription to "Folksy Plus".		
NuMonday	Smaller than Etsy again, but UK based. Stylish layout, similar to Etsy. They don't charge listing or transaction fees due to their pricing plans covering this.	Although they don't charge listing or transaction fees, if your sales don't cover the subscription fee then you could make a loss. They use Stripe, which is often considered to be a less reliable method than PayPal or bank transfers, for your payments. Only accept UK sellers, low global SERP ranking.
Payment using "pricing plan" packages, can be quite expensive if you don't make enough sales to cover this.		
British Craft House	Claiming to be "best of British", they use phrases like "artists" and "artisans" to try and promote high quality.	This site is smaller again, and less well known. We can't comment personally as neither of us have tried this platform, but the fees do seem quite expensive.
As above, subscription-style payments using "packages".		
ArtFire	Customers don't need to set up an account here to make a purchase, which will appeal to some customers who dislike obligatory account creation.	With ArtFire there is a limited ability to customise your shop and run promotions.
Three different tiers of payment plan to choose from, at $4.95, $20 and $40 per month.		

All information correct as understood at the time of writing.

information required to get your craft business up and running on the web in just a few easy steps.

Handmade marketplaces e.g. Etsy, Folksy and NuMonday

Handmade marketplaces are a great place to start, giving you instant access to thousands of shoppers already searching in your category. Simply put, the customers are already there looking for you. Sites like Etsy require no real understanding of website creation, allowing you to quickly list your products for sale, with photographs and a description for a small fee. Additionally, shoppers have more trust in a household name like Etsy, in comparison to an unknown new retailer. The downside of these craft marketplaces is that you can sometimes get lost within an already-saturated market (unless you opt to run paid ads), particularly since there are some mass-producers pretending to sell handmade items on there. Another downside is that there are limited options for a customised shopfront, unlike when you build your own website and can have the layout any style you like.

Mainstream online marketplaces e.g. eBay and Amazon

These have the same benefits as the handmade marketplaces in terms of their quick and easy-to-use design, with quick access to thousands of global customers, however they sell a wide range of pretty much any products you can think of, including from large-scale companies and mass producers, and don't have the unique vibe and particular audience that a website like Etsy has. In 2015, however, Amazon launched Amazon Handmade, designed to give crafters another platform to compete with the likes of Etsy. To sell on this, you must submit an artist application, which gives an air of exclusive authenticity preventing mass producers to claim their items are handmade. The downside of this is that it has an expensive monthly payment plan on top of the transaction fees and isn't well-known by many buyers. Products sold on Amazon Handmade do not show up in search results on the normal Amazon site (unless you specifically search using the term "handmade", or within the "Handmade"

Website Builders Pros and Cons		
Marketplace	Pros	Cons
Wix	Wix makes it really easy to build a beautiful website with intuitive drag-and-drop design tools and fantastic templates. It is a great choice for showcasing photography. There's a range of subscription types, ranging from a free basic website to a more costly eCommerce plan. This is one of the very best options for beginners and small businesses who want their own website.	You can't connect your own domain name or sell products without a paid subscription. If you do opt for a paid eCommerce plan, then it requires strong promotion to make sales. If you don't make any sales through this channel, then you may find it's not worth the payments - however this is generally the case for all paid online shop creators. With Wix, you must remember to optimise your pages for both desktop and mobile viewing, but this is fairly easily done.
SquareSpace	Great for creating content e.g. blogging. If you are a writer, influencer or photographer who creates a lot of content, then this may be a good option. It does provide options to connect payments for online selling, however this could confuse newbies!	Not purpose-built with eCommerce in mind, which should be a key objective if you are online to sell. Blogging and other long form content doesn't always drive sales, so don't invest too much time in it if it's not your main strength or goal.
Shopify	Created purely for eCommerce, Shopify has a lot of specialised web features - good for if you are selling hundreds of different types of products.	While useful, it seems that the wide range of features that Shopify provides isn't really necessary for a smaller business with a narrow product range, or for web beginners.
Weebly	Good functionality for slightly bigger shops as they have a greater capacity for dealing with a large number of web pages, but great for small businesses too as they have a fairly cheap starting plan and easy usability.	Features a smaller range of templates to choose from than Wix or SquareSpace, with a more limited range of drag-and-drop customisation abilities. It only allows customers to pay with PayPal if you use the highest-priced plan.
GoDaddy	This is reportedly a good option for when you need to create a website quickly and easily. It has a user-friendly interface, making it good for beginners.	GoDaddy has fewer design tools and other features than options such as Wix or SquareSpace have, making it a poorer choice for sellers with large product ranges and a desire for creative control.
WordPress	WordPress is a good choice for when you have a lot of written content to promote, such as a blog. lit has a huge range of customisable design features for your website, which allow for online selling too.	WordPress can involve some slightly more complex computing knowledge - a good option if you are already good at coding. Many of the customisable features and designs you will want are hidden behind a paywall, so additional costs must be factored in.

All information correct as understood at the time of writing.

category so, generally speaking, shoppers already have to be browsing Amazon Handmade goods to find you there.

Bear in mind that fees on this website may vary between private and business sellers. Therefore, if you are an absolute beginner, it may be worth testing the market and seeing if you can sell a couple of items as a private seller before you register as a business. If you make no sales during your designated test period, then you may not be ready to launch as an official business yet - or it may just be the wrong platform for you! It's okay to test out different platforms and see what works.

eCommerce Website Builders e.g. Wix, Squarespace and Shopify

The primary benefit of creating your own website is the freedom and flexibility over how your shop front and product listings look. These are great for building bespoke branding from homepage to checkout and can add an authoritative feel to your shop. These are incredibly easy to use, with attractive templates, drag-and-drop layout interfaces and online assistance for if you get stuck. The primary drawback of these is the fairly high monthly or yearly fees for full eCommerce abilities. Many providers, like Wix, do have options for a free basic website, but if you want to use your own domain name, have a shop, or have other more advanced business tools, the fees quickly add up. If you manage to draw enough interest and make enough sales, however, then any fees may be well worth it for your growing business.

Whichever option you choose, it can take quite a bit of work to start seeing results. And remember that what is best for someone else's business may not be what's best for your business. So be patient and stay open to learning and adapting as you go along. As we have previously suggested, it's OK to try out different things to see what does work, and you can always abandon what doesn't. See our comparison tables below for more information on each eCommerce platform.

Social media shops

More recent developments in eCommerce include the rise of social media shops - namely Shops on Instagram and Facebook Shop. These were created in response to the growing popularity of social media as a marketing tool, allowing customers to buy directly through social media accounts, rather than redirecting to an external source. Many customers already feel more comfortable shopping with a brand that has a strong online presence, and social media makes it easy for customers to share

comments, ask questions, and share your shops with their friends. These social media shops are not yet available in every country, and selling on them does incur a small fee. Despite this, they could be a particularly good option for businesses with a younger consumer base, and/or for businesses that are able to connect with relevant online communities via social media.

Still confused?

We can't tell you what to do - the right choice will be different for every business. However, if you are only just starting out and don't want to spend too much time or money on building a website, then why not test the water by listing a few products on Etsy, and seeing how much interest they get? This will help you get a feel for things before you start investing more in it. If you find you suddenly have a large number of orders and followers, then maybe branching out and investing in your own website will be a good idea. If you are unlikely to have the time or money to spend on making your own website work properly, then simply don't bother. A badly made website could do more harm than good to your brand, so try just using the pre-existing outlets instead.

Getting technical with your own website

Whether you are creating your own website or getting someone to do it for you, make sure you always retain an element of control. I've heard too many stories of people getting seemingly reasonably priced website designers on the case who can simply lock you out of your own site. You need the password for the hosting, for the management system for the payment system and the licenses for any add-ons you choose to buy. Don't get caught out. It can be an expensive and time-consuming mistake not to do so and could collapse your business if your designer goes bust, goes missing, or if you fall out. For this reason, creating your own simple but manageable website on a platform such as Wix or WordPress may actually be the best option to ensure full control over all areas.

There are several things to consider in order to avoid having one of "those" websites. We've all seen them and I'm not going to website shame here, but there are some design mistakes which could turn a potential customer off. I'm pretty easily irritated and not at all persistent when a website is not well designed for readability and function. I'm not unusual in this - in fact, most people have a low tolerance for poor websites when browsing. Looking after the minor irritations will keep your potential customers looking long enough for you to make that important sale. Turn a customer off in the first few seconds they may leave and never come back. After all there are ten more interesting things for them to look at. Some design may look artistic but not be fit for purpose. It's worth asking yourself if your target market can actually see small text at all. And don't start with lots of wordy introductions to your business and its philosophy. Plenty of time for that! And you can have a separate "about me" page. You want to get them straight to the "Ooh, ahh" moments. Always make sure that your site is easy to navigate and that it's obvious where they can find each category of product.

Personally, I absolutely hate lock screen advertising and cookie consent boxes. I will also back out of any website which, before they show me what I've clicked on, decides that they have a more important message to show me. I'm also likely to back out of a site which advertises one thing which suddenly isn't on the screen when I click and is replaced by the business' whole range which I then have to scroll through before finding the item which enticed me. Make it easy and pleasurable for your potential customer and they'll forget that they are busy and will come in and browse. Have a lovely bright image on your front page, but ensure it is compressed so it doesn't slow down your page loading speed. Personally, I'm a fan of white backgrounds to all your photographs. They lighten the mood and excite the eye. See more details on getting your product photography right for this back in Chapter 8.

Here in list form are the important things to remember when constructing your site or having it constructed for you. You can check these off when talking to a website designer or doing it yourself.

Website dos and don'ts

DO	include links to your other platforms somewhere at the top of each page, such as your various social media accounts, Etsy, Patreon, and anything else.
DON'T	go too over-the-top with design, using too many fonts or distracting patterns. Dark background colours with white or italic fonts can make your eyes dance, especially on smaller devices. Use something simple and easy to read throughout.
DO	make sure your website is optimised for both mobile and desktop viewing. People are shopping online using their mobile phones in increasing numbers, so you need to check that your website looks good on a narrow mobile phone screen, with navigational and call-to-action buttons easily visible towards the top of the screen, as well as pictures and text at the correct size. If you have a shop on a third party website like Etsy, you won't need to worry about this as the shop layout is pre-fixed, but if you use a website builder like Wix, you may want to look into mobile compatibility in more detail.
DON'T	make your page cluttered and confusing. Use a simple layout with a search tool and navigation bar that make it easy for shoppers to click through links, find what they want and take action, whether that is buying a product, signing up to your mailing list, or choosing to follow you on social media.
DO	create categories for products on your online shop, rather than cramming multiple product types onto one page. Not only does this simplify your layout, making a more attractive page for your customers to land on, but it has the added benefit of improving your SEO for each category and product. When each category and product listing is as specific as possible, this means you will attract more visitors looking for that exact thing. Conversely, if you cram everything into one page and use keyword stuffing, not only will search engines give you a lower position in their search results, but website visitors are more likely to be overwhelmed and navigate away in favour of finding a more specific and simplified experience elsewhere.
DON'T	use too many images or videos with large file sizes. You want your images to be as high-quality as possible but, before adding them to your website or online shop, use an easy, free online tool such as www.tinypng.com. You can import your images into there, and they will reduce the file size for you, so you can re-download it and add it to your website, without adding extra time onto your page load speed.

10. Improving your online sales

You have your beautiful products, your attractive website or your Etsy shop, So far we have only talked about where you are going to be seen and what you are going to show your potential customer when they 'wander' into your shop market stand or virtual shop. There's just one thing missing, customers! So, let's find some shall we? And not just a few customers but a lot of customers. And not just any old customers but the kind of customers who are excited by your products and interested in buying either now or in the future when their next paycheck comes. Motivated customers are the holy grail of marketing.

There are many ways to improve the performance of your online business. These mainly involve various methods of attracting an audience, which should organically increase your chances of making a sale. One primary route you should be taking to get your business seen online is to promote yourself via various forms of social media. There are several ways to do this, and engaging in these arenas is a quick way to provide potential customers with a link directly to your shop. This, however, is more specifically a marketing consideration, and is discussed in greater detail in Chapter 11.

For some specific aspects of eCommerce (online selling), a deeper understanding of how this platform works can really make a difference to your sales. Here, we provide an outline of some of the most important considerations for eCommerce, including how to write fantastic product descriptions that will get you found on Google. Bear in mind that this is an overview, designed to give you a well-rounded understanding of online selling for craft businesses. Each of these topics could warrant a whole guide of their own! So, once you have gotten started with the basics, you may wish to revisit each topic outlined and investigate in greater detail.

E-commerce Acronym Glossary

We know that acronyms are where most of us get stuck. Knowing what each of them stand for will give you a head start when learning about how to construct and market your craft business online. Don't let them

ACoS	Advertising Cost of Sale	This is a metric used by Amazon, measuring the performance of their Sponsored Products campaign. ACoS = £ cost of advertisement ÷ £ sales made.
AOV	Average Order Value	AOV is one key performance indicator to keep your eye on. This is pretty straightforward, referring to the average financial value of each customer order.
BR	Bounce Rate	Bounce rate refers to the number of visitors to your website who immediately leave after viewing just one page. You want to reduce your bounce rate and increase your conversion rate.
CPC	Cost Per Click	CPC refers to the amount you pay each time someone clicks on one of your PPC adverts. You want a low CPC in order to generate a high ROI.
CR	Conversion Rate	This defines the rate at which visitors to your online shop are converting into customers (i.e. buying from you).
CTA	Call To Action	A Call To Action is a point at which you encourage your customers to take action. Basic examples of this include: "buy now", "click here", "call today" and "sign up here", however writing these in a persuasive, non-pushy way is a skill that you can and should develop.
CTR	Click Through Rate	This basically refers to the percentage of impressions (aka views) of a website link or advertisement that resulted in a click. This percentage tells you how often people who see your ad or webpage end up clicking it. The formula is clicks ÷ impressions = CTR. So, if you have 10 clicks and 100 impressions, then your CTR is 10%.
CX or UX	Customer Experience or User Experience	These two terms mean very similar things, relating to how customers and users experience interactions with your website. You want to give them a positive user experience.

HTML	Hyper Text Markup Language	HTML is the language used to build websites. If you are solely selling through a third-party such as Etsy, or using a smart website builder such as Wix, you don't really need to know this. If you are building your own website from the ground up, however, some aspects of this will become important.
KPI	Key Performance Indicator	Key performance indicators are measurable determiners of progress/success. These include things like AOV (average order value), BR (bounce rate), CR (conversion rate), website traffic and total sales.
PPC	Pay Per Click	This is a form of internet advertising, in which you can run adverts to show on search engines or other websites. You pay a fee each time someone clicks on your ad.
ROI	Return On Investment	The ROI, or Return on Investment is all about making your money back. Ensuring you cover all costs, as well as make a profit, is key, so your ROI is a key point to look out for.
SEO	Search Engine Optimisation	Think of this as "findability". If your website is optimised for search engines, such as Google and Bing, this means that your business can be easily found by people who are searching for it, or for the products and services you have to offer.
SERP	Search Engine Results Page	This refers to the page of results that come up when looking for something using a search engine, such as Google. In an ideal world, your website will appear on the first SERP (e.g. page 1 of Google search results), without having to click to results page 2 or beyond.
URL	Uniform Resource Locator	The URL, also known as the web address, is the string of information used to locate a website, which also contains the domain name. The domain name is basically your website name. For example, the domain name of Google's search engine website is google.com. In the website address https://www.google.com/maps "google.com" is the domain name, and the rest of the information is the URL, providing the path to their specific "maps" page.
USP	Unique Selling Point(s)	Your USPs are the factors that appeal to your customers and set you apart from the competition. What do you offer that they don't? Why should people buy from you? What makes you and your business stand out? This is covered in branding, see Chapter 6.

scare you. You really don't need to know what they all mean immediately and can skim over it for now if you want to. Just know that this reference guide is here for you if and when these terms come up in the future. If you are getting help from a professional, at least now they won't bamboozle you. But don't be afraid to ask them what they mean if they come out with a new one.

How to get your business seen online

So far we've only talked about where you are going to be seen. Now we need to dig a bit deeper into how.

Search Engine Optimisation aka SEO

If you're not familiar with this term already, then don't be put off by the jargon-y feel. As discussed in the acronym glossary, you can think of SEO as "findability", or how easy it is for people to find you on the internet. This is less of a concern when selling through a third

party such as Etsy, but if you manage your own website then it is an important consideration.

Unless someone already knows your business name and website address, they are most likely to come across your website using a search engine, such as Google. Therefore, you want your website to appear as high up as possible on the search engine results pages (or SERP) when people search for your product type or services. For example: imagine you sell hand carved wooden birds. You want to make sure that when someone searches for the key phrase "hand carved wooden birds" on the internet, that your shop is one of the first results that they see. But how can you ensure this?

Just like in the discussion about whether to create your own website or outsource the work, search engine optimisation is a complex industry in itself and, if you have the means, it may be worth paying someone else to help you with this. At the time of writing, I believe that for somewhere between £100-£200, you can hire an SEO expert to analyse your website and provide clear advice on how you can improve. This is a great choice for somebody looking to invest and quickly build a strong online presence. On the other hand, if you are anything like us, you may wish to learn the nuts and bolts yourself and take a DIY approach.

While you don't need to know everything about SEO to run a successful online business, having a basic understanding of the key principles will help you to have a better website with more visitors in the modern competitive market. Understanding what SEO is and why it's important will help you to craft attractive and informative product pages that actually reach their target market.

Keywords: How to conduct keyword research

This is a really interesting subject when you feel ready to get a real handle on what drives people to your online shop. Don't let this subject frighten you if you've never come across it before. Just have a poke about until it starts to make sense. You'll find it an incredibly powerful tool to help you find out what your customers are looking for, how they are looking, and to make sure it's you that they find first.

Keywords are the pretty much most important consideration in SEO. In this context, "keywords" refers to the specific words and phrases that people use to search for products like yours. Think of each keyword you use as an opportunity to match with a shopper's search. Commonly searched for phrases, when specific and relevant to your business, are the ones that you want to be using in your product descriptions and throughout your online text, in order to connect with the people who are searching for them.

Keywords are also used on online marketplaces in various ways to improve the searchability of your products. When selling books on Amazon or Kindle, they have a "keywords" section, making it easy to add relevant keywords regarding your genre etc. When selling products on Etsy you have the option to add up to 13 product "tags", which again work in the same way as keywords on Amazon, to match your product with customer searches. These are a form of metadata, which is discussed further on. You can use the following advice on how to research and use keywords for a broad range of platforms, but you can always search online for more specific advice on your chosen marketplace.

To begin this journey, you must engage in some keyword research. Start by making a list of the main key terms you can think of related to your products and services, and then expand on them, thinking of all of the synonyms that other people might call the same product. For example, if you make soft canine shaped toys, are people more likely to be searching for "dog teddy", "plush dog" or "soft toy dog"? Finding out what keywords people search for most often allows you to cater to them, using those keywords on your web pages. Type some of the terms you have listed into Google and do some market research. What do other businesses and customers call similar products to yours? Be aware of language differences in the parts of the world you are targeting. For example, in the United States, your toy dog may be called a "dog plushie".

These keywords are to be used in various areas across your website or online shop, including the category title and descriptions, product descriptions, image captions, and generally any text you include. They are particularly important to consider when writing product descriptions (more on this below). Additionally, on many websites you can add listing "tags", which act as hidden search terms. They don't show up on your page, but they mean that your page should show up in search results when people search using those terms. This is why it is important that you understand precisely which terms people are using to search within your category, so that your business shows up for the most common and relevant searches.

To get an accurate gauge of what keywords you should be using, there are websites that can help you with this. One of our favourites is the Keyword Explorer tool from www.moz.com which is free for use - you need to make a login, but this service costs nothing, and you don't need to enter any bank details to use it. This helps you find out how many people search for a keyword in any given month and suggests alternative keywords you might want to use. This tool is great because you can look according to which country you're in and adjust the range of the results you wish to look at. There are plenty of online tutorials on how to do this, and Moz has a help page with a guide on how to use the keyword explorer here: https://moz.com/help/keyword-explorer/getting-started/overview

In brief, you simply enter one of the keywords from the list you have made into the Keyword Explorer search bar, and Moz will show you exactly how many people are searching for that term online per month and by location, as well as suggesting other related keywords that you may wish to use. You can then make a list or spreadsheets of these keywords and their search volumes to inform your online writing. Another popular alternative to Moz is www.ahrefs.com which also has some free tools, as well as more expensive subscription services.

Example:

Using our previous example, imagine that you want to sell handmade stuffed toy dachshunds. Your keyword research may look something like the below two columns on the left. I have included my own notes to the right of the keyword research to explain what the research on the left can teach us.

If you already have an online shop or website and want to improve it, in many cases you can find out what keywords are already being used to find you online and amend your product descriptions to include these. When selling on Etsy, for example, you can find data on your traffic sources (i.e. where people found your site). Using the Sell On Etsy app makes this information easy to see. Not only does this tell you where they are finding you (e.g. via Etsy search, Google search, Facebook, Twitter etc), it also has a section showing "Search Terms". These are the terms that people have been using to search when they have seen and clicked on your page. If there is a keyword or two that shows up more commonly than any other, then you should make sure you are always using these among your keywords, since you know that there are already a lot of people searching for them. For example, on my Etsy search terms list right now, it shows I have one term that has led to 73 visits recently, whereas all the other terms people have found me by have between 10 and 17 views. Therefore, I want to focus my attention on the one that has led to 73 shop visits.

Another way to gather data on your traffic sources and search terms is by setting up a Google Analytics (GA) account and connecting it to your online shop, whether this is an independent shop or an online marketplace like Etsy. GA is a free web analytics tool that tracks the traffic to your website and measures the behaviour of your website visitors, allowing you to see what is working and what isn't, so you can adjust accordingly. While GA is also mentioned in our "measuring your own marketing performance" section, this is slightly more advanced, and we don't want to overwhelm you from the beginning as this could be the topic of a whole other book. But it isn't too complicated at all, and it's very, very useful once you wrap your head around it.

Always make sure the keywords you choose are as specific as possible. For example: rather than titling your page "miniatures" (which is a little vague, making it hard to stand out), describe what is being sold on that page much more explicitly, such as "12th scale miniature vegetables" or "miniature hats for dolls". This will reach a smaller number of people who will be more likely to buy. Do check first whether there is any search volume for those phrases in Moz before using them, to make sure that you are catering to what people are actually searching for. a keyword is only valuable if it is a term that shoppers will actually be using when they search.

How to use your keyword research

For each of your web pages, whether it is a homepage, product page or any other, pick up to 3 main keywords, while choosing one primary one to focus on. Trying to optimise for too many things at once gives you a low "page authority" in the eyes of Google's algorithms and, therefore, you don't rank well for anything. The goal is to get a high page authority, meaning that Google sees your web page as having clear and concise enough information to grant you a top spot in search results. Focusing your attention on a smaller handful of keywords allows you to be more accurate and authoritative over your topic or product.

Make sure you use your chosen keywords often on each web page, using your primary keyword in both the title and the first line of your product description. See our section on "How to write product descriptions for the internet" section for more guidance on this, including our product page template, plus examples of good and bad product pages later in the chapter.

Having different categories and pages for your products allows you to better maximise optimisation opportunities for the specific phrases mentioned above. For example: if you sell miniature vegetables and miniature flowers, have separate pages for each of these so that you can focus your optimisation on a smaller handful of keywords for each page. This gives your page a higher authority, driving visitors to pages that more accurately reflect what they are looking for.

Beware keyword stuffing!

While you need to use your chosen keywords in as many places as possible on your web pages, if done badly, this can also work negatively against your search engine ranking. Google, for example, has clever algorithms which will analyse your website to make sure

Keyword Research

Keyword	Search Volume	Notes
soft toy dog	101-200	Great search volume to work with, but in search results your product will sit alongside soft toy labradors, schnauzers, corgis and more. Why not use the breed of dog, to reach a more precisely targeted audience?
soft toy dachshund	0	Poor choice as it has no search volume.
dachshund soft toy	11-50	This is a great example of why keyword research is important. Look at the search volume for this term compared with the one above. Just a slight tweak of the word order here allows you to connect with people who are searching using this phrase. You could even use this for your product title, but extend it to "Dachshund soft toy dog", as this will rank for the terms "dachsund soft toy" and "soft toy dog" simultaneously.
sausage dog	11.5k - 30.3k	Really high search volume, but too vague to bring in customers.
dachshund teddy	11-50	This seems like a good choice, but when searching for this term on Google it appears there is a high competition with Amazon, Argos, John Lewis, and other large companies, so you may be able to find a better match of keyword with lower competition.
giant sausage dog teddy	11-50	This is a great choice of keyword as it is very specific, and you know that the 11-50 people who search for it a month are actually looking for giant sausage dog teddies - not photos of sausage dogs, tiny sausage dog teddies, dachshunds on t-shirts, and so on.
sausage dog gifts	851-1.7k	Search volume too high - this term is too vague, making it hard to rank well against competition.
dachshund gifts	201-500	Same as above, far too vague. Interestingly, it does tell us that people searching in the gift category tend to use the term "sausage dog" more often than "dachshund".
toy dachshund	101-200	This may seem like a good choice, but this is an example of how a keyword can catch you out. There is a breed of dog called the Toy Dachshund - therefore, people searching for this term are likely to want information about the breed, rather than to purchase a handmade stuffed toy. This is also a good example of why, once you have selected some potential keywords, it is best to search for them in Google, to make sure they are accurate terms as well as to check out the competition for that keyword.
dachshund cuddly toy	11-50	Good choice.
dachshund plush	11-50	Good choice.
dachshund plush dog toy	11-50	Even better choice as using this would also allow you to rank for all three search terms: "daschund plush", "plush dog toy" and "daschund plush dog toy". There is still fairly high competition for this keyword, however as it is more specific, it will link you with a more specific audience.

it actually has some valuable content, and isn't simply stuffed full of keywords. You will probably have seen shops and websites with keyword stuffing before, and it occurs often in product titles on eBay. Keyword stuffing (also known as keyword density) is when a page doesn't have any real product description, and just lists a long string of alternative names for the same product. Google devalues pages like this, and they should show up lower in search results.

To avoid this, make sure that you have lots of valuable text surrounding your keywords - i.e. proper product descriptions with useful information. Use the keywords and phrases as part of longer chunks of text. Bullet points and tables are well received by Google, as these tend to contain useful information. If you get this right, you can sometimes achieve a "top spot" on Google. Ultimately, websites that appear as the first result in a search engine, or at least on the first page of results, are always more likely to get more visitors - you want this to be your website!

> **Takeaway**: Be specific with your language, particularly in your product title. Pick the most common/popular names for your product and use them throughout your product description. Pepper them into the image captions, and anywhere else you can add text to your online shop, without too much rambling or repetition.

How to write product descriptions for the internet

You don't have to be a born writer to craft a good product description. It is a skill that can be learned. It does, however, help to understand what keywords you need to be using, as discussed in the previous chapter. If you haven't read that bit yet, it will definitely be useful to have a look at it before moving on to this section.

Try to treat your product descriptions as though you were writing directly to your customer. Use full, concise sentences, but avoid rambling and unnecessary detail. Keep it to the point, while using descriptive words to make your product sound attractive. The more detail the better: the customer wants to know as much as possible in a short space of time. What is it made of? What size is it? Do you sell multiple varieties of the same product? Many of these details could be included in a table or bullet-point list of product specifications (which do also help your SEO). But get all the USPs into the main description. Is it extra-soft? Lifelike? Easy to use? Consider what you would want to know about the product if you were a customer, and what would persuade you to buy.

Ensure that you have selected some keywords that are specific to your product, and be sure to include them as part of your product descriptions so that potential customers can find you. Writing a longer product description allows you to use your keywords as much as possible, without risking a high keyword density.

At first it might seem a little robotic to try and fit your chosen keywords into the text. With a little practice this soon becomes second nature.

Finally, as mentioned in the previous section, it's important to remember that you want to have different text (such as different product titles and descriptions) on each web page, using different keywords. Using the same information on each page will do more harm than good. Treat each page and product with individual care.

Online product descriptions exercise

1	Pick one of your products to work with.
2	Write a list of potential keywords and try using the Moz keyword explorer tool to get an accurate understanding of the search volume (or traffic) for each word or phrase.
3	Pick the top 3 keywords for your product (with one primary keyword to focus on).
4	Use your primary keyword to write your product name (which should also be your page title).
5	Write a description for your product, and try to include your 3 keywords naturally in the text.
6	Assuming you will display at least 3 images of your product, write a caption for each image using your chosen keywords.

What to include on your product page

Product name

This should be your primary keyword, be as specific as possible, using your keyword research, as discussed earlier.

Alternative product name

You can also choose an alternative popular keyword. Depending on your layout, this could be included in the bullet points or image caption, or simply next to or underneath the main name/title.

Photographs

Include a good range but pick one primary "hero shot". Ensure these have rich captions and "alt text" (an image description in the backend which helps search engines to understand what your image is about, and can be read by screen readers for people with visual impairments, increasing accessibility) which is normally easy to do as part of the image upload process in most website builders.

Bullet points

Having bullet points of the features and benefits of your product is both useful to your customers, and favoured by search engines, however, this isn't always necessary or possible on marketplaces such as Etsy.

Description

A longer form description, including descriptive details of what it is, how it's made, and any other essential or persuasive information, including relevant keywords.

Metadata

This includes a page title and meta description for each individual page. The meta title shows in the "tab" section at the very top of your webpage within your

Good And Bad Examples Of Online Product Pages

	Good Example	Bad Example
Keywords	Donkey necklace, polymer clay donkey, donkey charm	Necklace, donkey, polymer clay
Images	Clear photo (with caption and alt. text), plus supporting photos	Blurry/dark photo with no caption or alt. text
Primary title	Polymer Clay Donkey Necklace	Necklace 1
Meta title	Polymer Clay Donkey Necklace | Donkey Charm Necklace	Animal necklace
Meta description	This Donkey Necklace with Polymer Clay Donkey Charm is handmade by *business name*, with realistic detail on a silver chain. Made to order in 3 size options.	No meta description
Bullet point 1	Donkey Necklace with Polymer Clay Donkey Charm	Necklace 1, animal necklace for sale
Bullet point 2	Handmade donkey necklace from *your business name*	This is a handmade product
Bullet point 3	Features a polymer clay donkey charm on a silver chain	Donkey with realistic detail, silver chain
Description	This Donkey Necklace is hand crafted with care in the UK from polymer clay. The polymer clay donkey is suspended by a narrow silver chain, finished with a lobster clasp. These donkey charms can be made to order and shipped within three to five business days.	This item is a necklace with a donkey on it made from polymer clay. These can be made in three to five business days

browser, and also in your search engine results. The meta description is the short blurb of text, around 157 characters maximum, that shows on the search engine results page - this is really important to encourage visitors to click on your link.

Clear pricing

Make the price quite clear so that customers don't have to hunt around, calculate VAT, or have to send a query about delivery costs.

Direct Calls-To-Action

Make the "add to cart" or "buy now" buttons clear and obvious. Elsewhere on the page you may also wish to prompt them to "click here for more information", "see more like this", or "sign up to my mailing list". On these pages you don't have to worry about coming across as too pushy or salesy in this way, as this is why shoppers are visiting you - giving a clear instruction like this simply helps them navigate the process and make decisions.

Online Shop Checklist	X ✔
Strong title	
Good description	
Use of up to 3 primary keywords throughout the above	
Multiple high quality product images to click through in an image gallery box (not in the main body of the page)	
Metadata	
Category sections	
FAQ section(s), with details such as material, sizing and delivery costs	
Clear calls-to-action (such as "add to Basket" or "click here for...")	
Clear pricing	

11. Social media marketing

Now you have all this information on making sure you know how to get the best possible coverage for your marketing (by using the right words and phrases and sprinkling them like fairy dust throughout anything and everything you put online), it's time to understand how building your "community" of fans and superfans will become a key component of your marketing strategy.

Social media is a key marketing consideration. This is not to say that you MUST get involved in this world if you're happy just selling at a few fairs, or selling to other shops and exhibitions. If you're happier with a slow life and don't need your business to grow, and your customers are mainly older browsers of shops and craft stalls, perhaps this isn't your primary focus. However, if you want to grow your business and keep your customers both feeling connected and becoming repeat buyers, it makes sense to build an online community of "superfans". Social media is a way to periodically keep your fans and customers interested.

Posting consistently and with care will help make sure that people love hearing from you as much as they love your work, and they will want to buy every time you make a call-to-action. A call-to-action, just to remind you, is when you subtly, or less subtly, say something along the lines of "join our mailing list", "download our guide" or the more direct "buy now".

You need to understand that social media is pretty transient unless you create something that goes viral or manage to rank highly for popular keywords, such as with hashtags. Because it's so fast-paced, you need to develop a sustainable strategy for being memorable and keeping people interested in your work, whether you post every day, once or twice a week, or less frequently.

Research shows that, on Facebook, posts with images get more interaction. Likewise, on Instagram, image captions that contain emojis are also likely to get you more engagement too. As with everything, once you've gotten to grips with the basics, you can begin to investigate the current trends for your chosen platforms.

Keep an eye on what response you get to your posts, and whether that results in more direct sales on your sites or more people visiting your stand at events. You can pay to run ads on most social media platforms now, which we have mentioned in the "start selling online" chapter. For the time being, however, we're mainly going to focus on posting to generate organic traffic.

> **Top tip**: *It may sound obvious, but make sure that you put the link to your shop on your social media page "bio" sections so that interested parties can quickly and easily go and buy from you.*

A note on hashtags and tagging

A hashtag, for the uninitiated, is simply a word or phrase with a hash symbol (#) preceding it, and these can point to content about that topic, it works a bit like a keyword. Users can search for particular hashtags, and save searches for their favourite hashtags, meaning that popular posts with these tags will show up in their newsfeeds. Hashtags must be all one word with no spaces, though you can have many words shoved together (e.g. #thisisalloneword). When you start typing in a hashtag to your image caption or comment, Instagram will show potentially related hashtags and their popularity in a dropdown menu, giving you more ideas of hashtags you could use.

Hashtags are popular primarily on Instagram, although they are used to a lesser extent on Twitter and Facebook. You can get away with littering your captions with plenty of relevant hashtags on Instagram, but only use one or two for Facebook and Twitter. Also, longer hashtags have been shown to be more popular for use on Facebook and Twitter, whereas varying lengths are all great for Instagram.

Hashtags are different to tagging, which refers to mentioning another social media user or account using their social media page name, preceded by the "@" symbol (such as @angiescarr). This provides a direct link to that users' page, and also notifies the person being tagged. Often people will "tag" their friends in posts that they want them to see. It can also help get your posts seen. For example, if you share a picture of yourself at an event like a fair, tag the official fair page, or the organisers. If you're using models and photographers to take pictures of your products, tag those models and photographers when you share those pictures. They will appreciate being linked to by you and may even share your post which may well win you more followers. However, tagging all your friends in a post advertising your or some other products is almost universally despised. Don't do it. It's likely to lose you friends and customers.

Social media platforms

As you can see in the following comparison chart, Instagram and Facebook are great venues for showcasing your work and building a community, respectively. Pinterest and YouTube, on the other hand, are useful for their longevity. Where Instagram and Facebook stories and posts are fleeting and hard to find on a news feed after a few days or even a few hours, YouTube and Pinterest work more like your page on an enormous and popular website. Their other USP is that they actually function more like search engines than social media. I had decided a few years ago that I didn't like Pinterest because it kept coming up on my Google searches and I couldn't remember my Pinterest password. I've re-evaluated it recently, however, especially in the light of how easy it is to use graphics from Canva to produce really attractive images, with the possibility of an embedded call to action. And of course, if it's coming up a lot on my searches, it's also coming up on those of my friends and customers'. YouTube is a great platform if you're able to keep up with producing video but, for me, Pinterest is quickly becoming one of my favourites thanks to a little talk by Naomi in the Small Business Networking Group on Facebook (both Naomi and the Small Business Networking Group are highly recommended).

3 rules for social media marketing: engage, add value, and be consistent

Engage

Firstly, you must post engaging content in order to attract any attention. Keeping people engaged with your social media content makes it easier to keep all your potential customers informed on all product developments, meaning they'll be ready to make a purchase whenever you're ready to sell. It also helps you to follow the trends of their behaviour. Listen to them. What are they talking about? What questions are they asking you? If you need inspiration for a new design, your followers will give you that and all it cost you was to listen to them. And they'll love you for it because everyone likes to be listened to!

When we talk about engaging with people on social media, however, it's not just about engaging them with your amazing content. Social media is all about participation. It's about communicating with other people and contributing to discussions yourself. When people comment on and share your work, comment back and thank them! You should also set aside a little time to regularly browse, search for new content, follow new people and other business, and like and comment on their posts. If it helps, think of this as online networking. Participating in this way helps to add that key element of personality, and engages people more with your business, as this makes it more personal.

The best way to stay connected is through online community building. There are lots of groups on Facebook for almost any kind of hobby or interest you can think of. Join these and contribute to them. If a group doesn't exist for your particular interest or craft type, this is a fantastic opportunity to create a group of your own (if you have the time to moderate a group, that is!). Networking through online interest groups is both more personal, and more instant. Within seconds, you can connect with thousands of people globally and if you stay up to date, you can also quickly piggyback on existing trends with your own message through hashtags, which are primarily popular on Instagram, as well as other social networks such as Twitter.

Add value

Always try to make your content relevant and valuable. You do occasionally want to post some "fluff" (i.e. light-hearted, attractive posts to add personality and interest beyond just promotional content), and to share content from others. Try to make the majority of your posts cohesive and relevant to your industry and your audience though. For example, if you are a teddy bear maker, don't spend a lot of time posting about your flower arranging hobby. There's no guarantee that your audience will be interested in seeing too many of these posts. You might bring in a lot of new followers, but if they're floristry enthusiasts and not teddy bear fans, then this isn't particularly valuable. Posts like these are unlikely to draw in new customers or lead to a sale. Instead, think about the type of content your customers might like to see. Give them some insight into your workspace or methods. Give them a sneak-peek of upcoming products or events. Tell them about other products or businesses that complement your own. Again, if you are a teddy bear maker for example, post links to or images of the work of teddy bear tailors, or teddy bear conventions and collections. This is the kind of thing your fans will like to see more of.

Be consistent

Post consistently in order to stay relevant, as social media is fast paced. It is easy for your content to get

SOCIAL MEDIA
The main platforms you need to know

FACEBOOK

Facebook is the most popular social media platform worldwide and it's easy to see why, since it makes posting and sharing so easy. It's primary benefit is that it reaches such a wide range of demographics, as well as the way it conveniently allows users to share any kind of posts with their friends, family and followers. The other benefit of using Facebook is the way that users can create and engage in both public and private groups related to their interests. Engaging with these relevant groups allows you to reach your target markets quickly, easily and freely.

INSTAGRAM

Instagram remains a firm favourite, particularly among younger users. It's a great choice for sharing quality images of your work. Users see a curated feed of posts by other users that they're following, or they can use a different option to see suggested posts that they may be interested in. A large benefit of marketing through Instagram is that users are more likely to search for topics using hashtags, so using these cleverly in your posts can get you seen by thousands of users.

TWITTER

Twitter is better for text posts, such as microblogging. It's not as useful for marketing or community building as some of the other social media networks, however if you're able to connect with your target market on there, then it can be particularly handy for developing your brand personality and for keeping your customers and fans informed about things like sales, events and even your personal life! Like Instagram, Twitter is also a good place to stay on top of trends.

YOUTUBE

YouTube is a video sharing site, and does class as a form of social media, although it may not look like it. It also functions in the same way as a search engine, allowing users to search for videos about specific topics. It was the 2nd most popular social network of 2020, so it is a good choice if you're up for making regular videos.

PINTEREST

Pinterest is popular for its longevity and link-building. Users share links on "boards" (like a virtual pinboard) on topic themes, so it's very useful for crafters, and these "pins" can be updated whenever you want. Like YouTube, it also functions in the same way as a search engine, as well as providing direct links to your pages, so it's great publicity if you can get people sharing your work on it.

LINKEDIN

LinkedIn is generally used as a professional networking site for business. As such, it has more of a business-to-business feel, rather than a business-to-customer feel, however, it can be good for establishing yourself as a professional and for getting involved in groups that are specific to your field.

lost in the onslaught of daily posts from others. Posting with a fairly consistent regularity and authority helps to increase brand awareness, so that your brand becomes recognized. Posting with a consistent style helps you to construct a strong brand identity, so that your business becomes recognisable by the type of posts that you share. Conversely, if you don't post at all for weeks and then post 10 or 20 times in one day, this kind of inconsistency could be irritating and doesn't help people to connect with you or your brand.

thing less relevant, but still attractive. For example, you could post a picture or piece of text about your holiday, pets, or baking achievements, to add a bit of personality and entertainment. You don't have to follow these rules strictly. Rules are not for everyone. They do serve as a good reminder to ensure that your social media presence is varied and entertaining and authentic, rather than being repetitive and sales heavy.

"What should I post?"

Various social media marketing experts have developed their own content ratio strategies to explain what type of things you should be posting, such as the 5-3-2 rule. This rule suggests that 50% of your posts should be sharing relevant content you have curated from others, 30% should be marketing content about your own business, and 20% should be personal content. There are many variations on this rule but, generally speaking, they all tell us that you should be aiming to have a balance between posting your own promotional work and sharing relevant content from others. Add in some light interjections of personal or fun content, such as a picture of your workspace or some-

Personal / fun content 20%

Curated content 50%

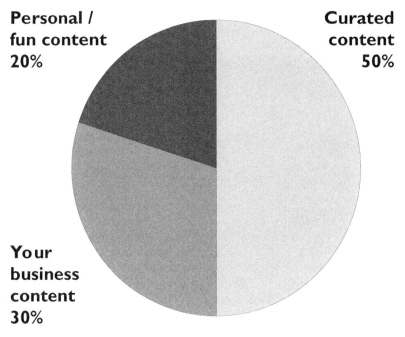

Your business content 30%

Make sure you know what the purpose of today's post is. Do you want your customers to buy today, or do you want them to be ready to buy next week? If you just want to keep them onside, give them something. It doesn't have to be a big 'gift'. Just a snippet of inspiration will be nice to receive. It costs you very little to keep your followers happy. From time to time it could be something more tangible. Perhaps you could give them a little tutorial or a PDF for a card or a photograph. Then, when you are ready to make an offer that your customers are likely to buy, they are ready. to do so. They know you to be generous, but they also know that occasionally you have to ask to be paid for something. They are very ready to be that customer. Especially when what you are selling is beautiful and desirable and comes from the lovely person that you are.

"How regularly should I post?"

Whatever you decide, you need to keep it consistent and achievable. If you start posting every day and gather an engaged audience, only to tire of it after a month, perhaps you should have started scheduling fewer posts over a longer period. You need to keep something fresh to keep your followers interested. Forced daily posts feel forced. They certainly put me off. I can recognise a forced daily inspirational quote a mile off, and they really are a turnoff for most intelligent followers.

Consider what you're able to keep up with. Do you really need to use ALL of the social media platforms? For a smaller business this is simply unsustainable. You really need to concentrate on which one, or two will work best for you. You can have a presence on the rest, but you need to make it clear which your main platforms are. Also, the ones you choose may be dependent on your target audience. It's well worth timetabling a morning as your marketing strategy morning to look at social media statistics as they relate to your target groups. If your appeal is across the board, you may wish to consider investing in an app which will post across the others automatically for you. Free social media scheduling software is available, such as IFTTT, which can help you to schedule posts and automate posting across all platforms. This will be useful if you find that you want or need to post a lot, and across all platforms - but not really necessary if you just stick with one or two.

Ideally, to save yourself time in the long term, and to ensure you have a clear idea and comprehensive strategy about where you are going, you should create a content calendar. You can use a normal calendar, either on your phone, computer, or you could even go "analogue" and use a pen and paper! As mentioned above in the case of IFTTT, if you want to get technical, you can use free apps to help schedule these posts for you ahead of time.

Bright ads for dull days

It's a good idea to prepare for those days when you want your social media posts to "pop", perhaps if you're needing a boost in sales. Our advice is to spend a day making up a folder of gorgeous images and composites of your most popular work, some of your best selfies and any old advertising that has worked very well before as well as any lovely reviews or feedback you've received. Make a habit, when someone gives you a really great review, of asking them if you can use it with or without their name attached. Keep it in your advertising materials folder. Look at other people's great advertising for inspiration. What is it about their ads that grabbed you? Start to make a list of ideas (or create a Pinterest board), and keep these in the bag for those days when inspiration is low.

If creating brand new content for social media seems like more effort than you've got time for right now, do remember that anything you write, or have written, can be recycled and repurposed. You may be working on a book at the same time, and your social media postings may reflect the outpourings of your overheated brain. Perhaps you can simply post a photograph of your work in progress, or details about how you made something. Any popular posts can be repeated or tweaked to produce a similarly interesting post. A successful theme can be re-used to produce a video or a webinar and vice versa. A popular video can be written as a pdf or part of a book. Don't forget magazine articles too.

If you make all of your work perform for you more than once, you bring your costs down and your profits up. Time is the most valuable asset of all, so don't waste it on the vague possibility of a few sales only.

"How do I build followers?"

If you're looking at your social media account and seeing tumbleweed, with very few followers or engagement from others, you may need to step up the way you're engaging with it. Simply posting good content isn't enough, you need to get out there and interact in order to be seen. Many social media users, particularly on Instagram, have a "like for like" or "follow-for-follow" culture, in that it is often considered polite to follow someone who follows you. Many users will go through the lists of people who follow similar brands, and then follow these users. This will often result in these users following you back.

Another method to increase your reach if you already do have a handful of followers, is to run competitions. Competitions on social media are most often designed to get your business shared by as many people as possible. A common method is to ask people entering the competition to follow your page, like a particular photo and share it. Then you pick one of these followers at random as the winner.

Asking questions is a great way of making your community aware of an upcoming product and perhaps ready to buy when it's released. Many authors, for example, will ask what you think of their book cover or get you to help choose between options. You can do the same with the style of buttons on a coat, or two different shades of the same piece of pottery. This really engages the reader and serves the double purpose of market research and advertising.

Engaging people this way is great for business, as the social network algorithms make it so popular posts are more likely to be seen by a wider audience. Additionally, it's worth bearing in mind that networking in this way can really make you friends in high places. If you truly engage with your audience and provide great content and products, you can get your work seen and talked about by magazine editors, retailers and even celebrities, without ever having to pay a penny on advertising costs.

When it's time to step it up, you can create what's called a 'lead magnet'. If you have a piece of shareable content that you can afford to give away. You can then say, "If you want this PDF (or whatever), please join our mailing list". Make sure you don't do too many freebies, though, or you will only end up with people who don't want to pay for anything. These are not your target market.

Anecdotally, we did recently share an ebook giveaway to remind everyone that I have books for sale and this one coming up and surprisingly I sold nearly as many as I gave away. So, don't be afraid of a well-targeted giveaway. I would never have got as much traffic at a similar spend in online advertising.

Social media etiquette: top tips

There are a few basic aspects of social media etiquette to be aware of. We won't labour this point, as it all comes down to basic politeness, really!

- *Credit others when you share their work.*
- *Thank people when they share yours.*
- *Separate your business and personal pages but do add personality to your business page.*
- *Don't "like" your own posts.*
- *This is the golden rule: always be polite (yes, even when somebody is upsetting you!*

> *Watch my video about how to measure, for your halloween costume! And don't forget to subscribe to my channel!*

Live messages, videos, "stories"

Video is an excellent way of bringing your personality into peoples' homes. I think I read the storybook rule that if you don't invite a vampire into your home you are safe from him (or her). Video is a bit like that. People invite you into their homes and so they are open to your 'advances.' It's a good job you don't want blood out of them. Just a healthy order.

People really are much more receptive to your sales pitch on video because they asked you for it. This is how YouTube makes its money, by tapping into this enormously receptive market. I'm not a big fan of Facebook and Instagram Stories personally, but they do provide a quick way of getting your content seen. Then there are Facebook Live sessions. I've used these. They help you connect with your community. Your community is made up of your best customers and supporters and friends. The same applies here as applies to fairs. People love to connect with their idols, their tutors, the people who wrote their favourite book or whose work they admire.

A video of you making something has a multi-level sales function. It sells the item directly from the admiration of the viewer who is in awe of your beautiful and cleverly made item. This also makes it a fantastic thing to post on all platforms. People are just itching to discover and share interesting content. It also brings in students who want to learn from you, if that's part of your business. One important thing to remember: avoid copyrighted music like the plague. Using unauthorised music could cost you your business. There are music-generating apps you can use, public domain music available or why not commission a friendly musician to do some for you?

Social media community as support for you and your business

"Some of this is confusing to start out with. How can I ease my way in?"

Support groups for small businesses can be extremely valuable. You have to be aware, of course, that many business group admins do have the groups as a front for marketing their business, but this isn't necessarily cynical. In the case of a Facebook group, I've found very valuable, Small Business Networking, the income stream grew out of the support group and not the other way around. You can join these groups in the full knowledge that there is going to be some advertising going on but as long as it's not strongarm tactics. You can take what you need and choose to join or not to join in paid levels. Personally, I rarely buy into the paid services, but that's not to say never. I'm just a resistant customer.

I have watched quite a few talks and taken a lot of entry level classes for free via these groups, and found them very useful. The rest of the group members can be people just like you and very supportive. Those that have caring admins seem to do best anyway so that tells you something about them. There is a problem with very large groups, as your posts and comments can be very quickly lost. In a good thread, your own support of other people will stand you in good stead. There's a lot of free learning on groups like this so make sure you join a few and see where you are happy. And try to give as much as you receive.

Top tips for group and network posting

See your groups as part of your community, which in turn is part of a wider creative community that includes other creators like you. If you give, you get. Try to forget all you've been told about giving without any hope of return and concentrate more on finding the win-win scenarios where you both give and get support that helps both of you. That said, give more frequently than you ask. Give value to your customers before you ask for anything back. In addition to the "5-3-2" rule above, regarding posts on your own page, if you're working on building community networks or posting in someone else's space, a general rule might be to share information 15 or 20 times before you ask for something. This depends how often you interact. If you are chatting less regularly, say, once a week, you might wish to make a "call to action" post just once a month. If you post twice a day, you could have a day of the week when you would have your product promotion day. We all know businesses that spam every day. It's uncomfortable and it turns people right off. You want your customers to be waiting eagerly for your next post because it makes them feel good. Social media is about how you make people feel. This leads on to my second point...

Spread the love. Not only does it feel good to have a business with a heart, but social media karma really does come back to you. What actually comes back to you is relevance. Your products will be listed in the "also-bought'" on certain platforms, and those lovely people whose work you promote will also promote you. That's the artist's way. There are still some who don't understand this, but they do mark themselves out by their reluctance to share their space. Those who are fearful of competition will build a cold wall around themselves that even the customer won't want to go through. So, think of supporting your fellow crafters as a reciprocal act, paying upfront as often as not. Obviously, you do have to like the person and their work to promote it but in the creative world that's not difficult. More often than not those people are just like you with similar hopes, fears and problems. What a lot of people forget is that customers generally don't buy only one of a type of item. If they buy from your community, they will probably buy from you too and even if they don't, reciprocity means another customer brought in by your friend will.

As mentioned in the "How do I build followers?" section above, question asking and answering can really be an effective tool in building your network of both support and potential customers especially when your product meets the needs of the group members.

Don't fall into the habit of posting irrelevant, mass-generated content just in order to have something to post. I've bought a content calendar to see if it would help with my planning. It reminded me to think about timetabling my posts, but some of the suggestions came across as a little "cheesy". I soon started to notice these clichés coming up on other people's posts, and your customers will too. They know you bought them from "inspirational quotes R us". You will get engagement on these posts, just not from the right people, and this consumes your time for no reward. Worse, you will alienate your friends and some of your best customers. Unless, of course, your ideal customer is the sort that likes a daily dose of bland.

Online security and general online health

Do remember, no matter who you are, almost all of your details, every word you say and picture you post can and is being recorded forever! People haven't yet got the idea that sometimes we all say things that we don't mean. Most of us change our minds with age and experience, so be careful what you post. A careless post can cost people whole careers. Always be sure of your facts. Always be sure of any copyright issues and just generally make sure you don't wilfully upset people. There are those who are always upset. You can't do anything about them. Don't rise to the bait and understand that sometimes the best policy is not to reply to rude online comments and "trolling". Someone else with less to lose will usually take them on for you and save you the trouble. Remember the passage of time won't save you from some stupid thing you might once have said. You can delete it, but it's never really gone. If you can't stand by it, don't say it. I'd advise you to not drink and post either, especially if you're the argumentative sort.

12. Customer service

Your customer service can make or break your business. Good news travels fast and, if you provide a great customer experience, those customers are more likely to leave positive reviews online and recommend you to their friends. Likewise, if you provide a terrible customer service, then you will accumulate negative reviews. Good and bad reviews can have a huge impact on the future of your business as they can stick around and affect your rating and ranking for years to come - you want to make sure that it's all positive!

5 ways to provide good customer service

Be approachable. While you want to try and pre-empt any obvious FAQ in your product descriptions and so on, provide clear contact options so that they don't have any hesitancy in contacting or ordering from you.

Respond to queries in a friendly, helpful and timely manner. Make sure your responses are punctual and friendly, whether you're responding to an email, a message or comment on social media, a phone call, or even dealing with customers face-to-face. Be personable, rather than robotic - making a real human connection can work wonders for your business/customer relationship.

Provide little extras where possible - send unexpected freebies out in parcels or hand out samples at events. These don't have to be expensive things - something as small as a sticker or a bag of sweets can really enhance the experience for your customer. The added benefit of giving them free branded goods, such as stickers with your brand logo on, is that it is free advertising for you, if they like it and choose to display it.

Encourage customers to leave positive reviews if they do like your products and service. Including a standard printed-out note in your parcel asking for positive feedback is fairly common.

Be prepared to listen and respond politely if they have criticism or negative feedback.

Dealing with complaints

Remember that, if you get a healthy sized order for something expensive to post, there is many a slip in this process. Customers can simply change their minds and refuse to accept a parcel, leaving you with the unexpectedly returned item and a very large bill for postage in some cases. An artist friend of ours recently had a healthy order for a canvas. Great, right? Only she suddenly found the shipping costs would be $500 from the UK to the USA. Of course, this wouldn't be good for either of them, so she rapidly renegotiated to send the canvas out of its frame and rolled into a postal tube. Still reasonably expensive if there was a problem, but a better shipping price for the customer and less chance of loss for her.

Always try to build into your prices the possibility of loss. Usually, it's not your customers fault if they aren't in when your parcel arrives, and the courier is too lazy to try again and simply bounces it. Complain to the courier but, basically, this is likely to be a loss, in the short term at least. You do need to resend or refund without question if there is a return to sender note and if there is no reason to distrust the customer. Don't make them wait until the postal service has taken its own sweet time to return the parcel. They are just as distressed as you, and it's their money. Plus, they are eager to see their goods! They will love you for understanding that and going the extra mile, this kind of customer service really makes a difference and can turn an unhappy customer into a much happier one.

One precautionary measure, which could save you and your customers a lot of headaches, is always to send your parcels with tracking. This is especially important if they are overseas customers. It does cost a little more, but if you factor that into your pricing, you will thank yourself later. With a tracking number, your customers can check the progress of the parcel themselves. They will see that you have posted it in time and that it is out of your hands and with the courier. Plus, if anything goes wrong you are able quickly to verify and rectify the situation.

It is understandable that, if you are posting very small, low-value items within your country, it may not be necessary to always pay extra for tracked postage. In this case, however, you must acknowledge that sometimes things will go missing or be delayed with no explanation. Because of this, in the case of very high-value items that are not easy to replace, I would always recommend that you ask your customers to pay for recorded delivery or even insurance - they will understand this, as they don't want their item to go missing either!

None of us are perfect, and it is possible that from time to time you may receive a complaint about an imperfect or damaged item. The customer is often correct in this case and, if so, it is always the best policy to own up and refund or replace the item or both! Ask them for photos so that you can understand what's gone wrong, and always be polite, even if they are rude. Maintaining the satisfaction of your customers is really important to your business.

An example from my experience is a time when, during a busy period in the middle of the COVID-19 pandemic, I had to switch to using a new supplier for some metal fastenings. I unfortunately didn't realise that they weren't the same quality as my previous supplies, and soon received a complaint that an item wasn't up to scratch and damaged on first use. I immediately refunded the customer and sent them a replacement part so that they could get their item working again. I also rectified the issue with my supplier. This resulted in a surprised and happy customer, who then left me a glowing review. Worth it!

There is a commonly used phrase "a complaint is a gift". This is true. Looking at the positives, you could pay more for less helpful business appraisal.

Let's acknowledge, however, that receiving complaints can really take the wind out of your sails. There are many people in this world who will rush to leave a bad review without first contacting you, or who can be rude and even cruel in their complaints. These cases may require more careful consideration and may unfortunately need to be put in the category of "difficult customers". There is always a way to handle them and you certainly shouldn't rush to judgement. Stop. Think. Take a deep breath. Move on.

Dealing with "difficult" customers

You have developed your lovely business personality. Mostly, it comes quite naturally to you to go that extra mile for a customer who seems to need that little bit more. But what do you do when a customer pushes you beyond your tolerance? Quite simply, you have to learn to say a kind but firm no to any customers who fall into the neither profitable nor a pleasure to deal with category. You may need to learn to say no even to those who are a pleasure to deal with, if they are affecting your income negatively.

There will be times that you get what we might call a "difficult" customer. Despite this, be sure never to prejudge or label your customers, because you never know when an initially tricky customer can become a really good one, if you give that extra bit of care to them. Sometimes they are just nervous and need to trust you. So, don't label a customer 'difficult' unless they truly do deserve the label, and then there are things you can do. The sad truth, however, is that there will be one or two cases where the customer is not as nice as they at first appeared to be. Getting too wound up is less healthy than building in a reserve to cover losses. Do all you can within reason, but sometimes it's time to let go, for your own benefit as much as theirs.

We've all had customers who start asking "where's my parcel?" the moment they have paid. There are those who start asking critical questions about the item once it has already been sent. Others who leave bad reviews for something being damaged in the post, even when happily and promptly replaced for free. Even if you have a pretty high tolerance level, there can come a point at which that tolerance is about to snap. You need to have a plan for these situations because that one customer can also do a lot of damage to your business. You can spend ten years building up a reputation for good customer service and one disgruntled customer can wilfully do a lot of damage.

When you receive any kind of complaint, always stay calm, and take a little while to collect your thoughts before you respond. You have to decide whether it is a legitimate complaint and it's time to apologise and refund or replace, or whether the customer is actually being unreasonable. And, in almost all cases, refund/replace is the best option. So my message to the "still waiting" customer is to always acknowledge their frustration and apologise for the slowness of the mail but to suggest that we wait until that time arrives, and state that of course we will simply refund if there is a loss in the post. This approach has never failed me, but I advise adding one more little boundary to this: that customer always pays for recorded delivery if they order in the future.

Be as pleasant and understanding as you can be, even in the face of rudeness. Adding a human dimension, rather than coming off as a faceless company, can work wonders. If their messages become aggressive or harassing, at some point you will have to put your foot down. Do always try to remain composed, however, as an angry backlash could damage your reputation permanently. It's crucial to prioritise customer satisfaction. Better off making a slight loss than getting bad reviews against your name.

If you get a high volume of tricky customers, it may be worth outsourcing the distribution and/or customer service work. When my business was very busy back in the "noughties", I developed a system of passing my exasperating customers over to one of my wholesale customers to deal with. I then only got half of the income, but I offloaded 100% of the hassle. My sweet friend was buying my products wholesale at a 50% discount. This seems generous, but she was better at maintaining the sweetness factor while I was overworked, and she was happy to have the work. She knew exactly what kind of exasperation she was going to have to deal with to earn her 50%. This was worth it for both of us.

Find your way of dealing with the 1% of customers who are really needy or unpleasant and set boundaries for yourself. How much are you prepared to do before you pass this customer over? Try to remember that all of your customers are real people with real problems of their own, and it pays to be kind. But, once your predetermined boundary has been crossed, it also pays to have a firm cut off point. This helps you to give 100% to the rest. We could count on one of our four hands customers who have ever passed this point, but between us we have traded for nearly 40 years!

Takeaway: Providing fab customer service across the board is so important because it will continue to benefit you in the future. Spending a little extra time or money on connecting with your customers and solving any problems with good faith will save you from those dreaded bad reviews, and make your customers more likely to recommend you to others.

Commissions and Custom Orders

When deciding to take commissions for custom orders, you must consider whether you have the time and materials available to make unique items on request. It may be the case that your schedule requires you to batch make items in advance, with no free time for special requests. Indeed, this kind of order can often be more time consuming, as customers will want to communicate with you in more detail about the specifics of their requests. This can sometimes turn into a lengthy back-and-forth of messages. And sometimes you can begin working on a commission, only for the customer to change their mind and cancel the order or decide that they don't like what you've made for them.

For the above reasons, it can be a good idea to build in terms and conditions for creating bespoke orders, such as allowing a longer turnaround time and, taking money upfront, and not accepting cancellations.

I had a lovely response to a question on a miniaturists' group, about taking commissions from customers. One lady said that when someone asks if she will make something for them, then she usually says yes, but always bears in mind that the person may not like the finished item and so she makes it her own way with the intention of simply giving the initial customer first refusal and being equally happy to put the work into stock. It takes away all the pressure of trying to please.

Another respondent told me that modeler & diorama maker Sheperd Paine used to say "I don't do commissions. But I do take suggestions". Which sounds like a really healthy attitude to me.

Of course, some of your businesses will be entirely on commission. There is something inherently marketable about bespoke goods. If you can build into your product an easy way to customise it for your customers, this could be a highly lucrative option, as people value uniqueness. For example, if you make clothing or accessories, offer the same item in a range of colours, or with various options for trimmings such as zips and buttons. If commissions are more difficult for you to do, but they're something your customers really want, then charge more for them to make it worth your while.

13. More on marketing

Creating graphics and using templates with Canva

We're big fans of Canva although it's new to me. Canva is a graphic design platform, used to create social media graphics, presentations, posters, documents and all sorts of other visual content. Canva also has a calendar function to allow you to work on graphics for future dates. It's free at the trial level but we have both moved on to using the professional version because you get extra features that we do feel are worth having. Especially if you work closely with other people. You can often get a free offer to create a small team without extra charge. We have our family in on ours. If you're a real novice and you need some help there are people who specialise in making Canva templates for you to tweak with your own name etc. It's extremely useful to make engaging elements for your social media posts that can even include video elements. It's also good for knocking out ideas for designs that you can then pass on to professional designers to refine. Kira has used it for a while to make mockups to pass on to the graphics guy at her work and I've just started doing that here in this book. I took my husband a Canva design for a vampire that was the jump-off for our own design. We worked on it on another platform to make our cute vampire.

Top tip: get a strategy! Think about upcoming product launches you will be doing. Any photography, events or any other promotions you have planned and begin to think about how and

when you might want to post about them on social media. Then, using the content ratios to give you a little guidance on how much you should be posting of each type of content, begin to fill in the dates on your calendar with reminders of what you want to be posting. Using Canva could help with this.

"Blogging: Is it worth the effort?"

The value of blogging varies depending on who you are, and what you do. Some people might argue that blogging as a marketing tool is a waste of time nowadays, and to some extent that is true. Longform blogging did have its heyday in the nineties and noughties. But that doesn't mean that blogging is dead; in many cases it has morphed into a new form. Social media posts are the new way to blog and communicate with people in a quick and easy manner. In the case of sites like Twitter, you have a character limit on what you can write, and this short-form posting style is often referred to as "microblogging".

I did try to keep a blog at one time, but found the work it took to keep writing it, promoting it and tracking its progress simply didn't result in enough pageviews or sales to be worth the thought or time, and it seems that effort is better spent on creating content for social networks. This may not be the case for everyone, and it doesn't mean that there's no need to keep a blog anymore, or that nobody will read it. A well-written blog that considers SEO and includes calls-to-action can still be a useful addition to your business, particularly if you are a writer who wants to showcase their writing skills in relation to their business. Blogs can help drive traffic to your website, but you have to make sure that they are converting readers into customers, otherwise it may well be a waste of your time. If you do begin a blog, aim to keep track of how many views you get and how many sales you might make in relation to when you are posting your blogs (Google Analytics can help with this).

Consider blogging only for those who want it, such as sending blog-style updates to those who sign up to your mailing list

Ooh, lovely Canva speech bubble!

or who sponsor you on websites such as Patreon. And do look at your social media output as a shortform style of blogging, which may reduce your need to spend time building an additional blog elsewhere.

Top tip: You can gather up your daily posts from other platforms and repurpose them as a blog, or vice versa.

Mailing lists

One of your earliest and most obvious calls to action would be a request for people to join your new data compliant mailing list. Many of us lost decades worth of work on mailing lists in the big data compliance shake up. Even though this was not the intention, it was almost like a land-grab by younger businesses who were data-savvy, from older ones who had put in the work but then lost their customer base almost overnight. I empathise with older businesses over this. I had a huge email mailing list which is now defunct. Now, we just have to knuckle down and start again. At least we can now find most of our customers again on social media.

"Why do I need a mailing list?"

A mailing list is a direct connection to your most loyal and engaged customers. In the craft world this can mean being as important as connecting with those 'fans' when you want to ask them to buy right now because you need to boost your cash flow. Or it can be just to keep them up to date with what you're doing when it might be lost in the hubbub and low lifespan of most social media. Yes we've mentioned that social media has a long memory for your mistakes. But it's woefully short for your successes. Also a lot of traditional craft lovers are turned off by social media and won't even see your news. You can collect their email addresses at fairs and exhibitions, or through magazine offers, etc. That is the one time I would consider advertising in a magazine. To regenerate your mailing list If your fanbase falls into the over 50s most of whom have email, but not all use social media.

"How do I start?"

A first step might be to mention on social media that you're starting your mailing list back up again and asking if they would like to be on it. Then, a very good device for bringing in an engaged group of people to your mailing list is to use a lead magnet. A lead magnet is something you give away for free in order to draw your customer in to allowing you to put him/her on your mailing list. This sounds cynical but used well, and targeted precisely it only brings in people who really do want to hear about your next product. This is very easy to do for businesses who trade in information, support, mentoring etc. It's more difficult for crafters who deal in traditional craft products. You can't simply be posting freebies round the world. You can however offer some other tangible benefit such as discounts or information. A hook and needle size guide from a knitter or crocheter who also sells yarn. An artist may release a downloadable print. A miniaturist may give away a tutorial.

Make sure your giveaways are totally relevant to the products that you want to sell so that they target only those people who are likely to open your mail regularly. Email addresses where the mail is regularly unread are a drain on your reputation with the email servers and email clients. Make sure that your customers are opening, reading and replying to your emails by giving them great reasons to do so. Make them feel special and connected once they have generously let you walk into their lives. Services like Mailchimp, Madmini etc. will lead you through the process. Most of these services are free at the very small business level. There are YouTube videos showing you how to use them. Make sure you don't keep data without your customer's permission and make sure their data is safe. We have several separate lists because my business has multiple layers from miniature collectors, to makers and those who are interested in different tools for different techniques. Those who want to come to classes or who want to read all my books. And we have a top level called 'Superfan'. Customers choose what information they want to receive. Make sure you give a clear unsubscribe option. Losing a subscriber who is not engaged is not a failure. It can be an actual benefit. Let your email subscribers know how regularly they are likely to hear from you. My superfans will hear regularly. The collectors will only want to hear when I have a whole new collection to show them. and the book subscribers only when I release a new book. That may only be once or twice a year.

14. Free and paid advertising

"I'm just starting as a business; I can't afford to advertise! Apart from using social media, what else can I do to get seen?"

Free Advertising

Catching the eye of the magazines

This may happen organically just because your work is so good, so innovative, so charming and so are you. But it doesn't hurt to give a little push to get people talking about you. Get them wanting to be the first to have noticed you, or your work and wanting to be seen with you. Wanting to share your posts and recommend you and your work. I only know these tricks because they happened to me by accident, over time, but you can take steps to ensure that it happens for you sooner rather than later. It's good to have your work profiled in a craft magazine, but this can only happen in each magazine perhaps once a decade. So, it's a nice little push but doesn't keep you in the public eye.

Are your photographs good, and do people want to make what you make? Can you share some of your secrets? Could you write step-by-step how-to projects for magazines? This is my favourite and the easiest way of getting a name for yourself. Magazines are always on the lookout for good quality content. Contact your favourite magazine and pitch your idea. Make sure you send a fully formed, ready to go project. Give them a timeframe to accept or reject it. In the unlikely event that they reject, look at what they may have rejected it for. Just alter it slightly if necessary and take it to the next magazine. If your work is good and appealing and covers two to four pages of their magazine, you're like gold to them and for you it's the best advertising possible. The drawbacks are that you're unlikely to get paid for your piece as a newbie. And, of course, you've now given away one of your ideas. The positives are the extra visibility of you, your brand and your work. You are now a minor celeb, "as seen in Lovely-Crafts magazine".

Here's another tip on the back of this one, and be very firm about this. Write a very clear statement to the publisher specifically reserving the right to republish your own work in any future book or online class you may produce. You can also ask them to request permission from you before allowing any sister publication to re-publish it. If you don't make that very clear, your work can be cheekily republished in their magazine in another country, just as you're trying to cultivate a relationship with a different magazine. This has happened to me. It's very embarrassing. Once you have a relationship, you can then ask for payment for your articles if they're popular and are bringing in extra readers. Because magazines are under pressure, however, your work will have to be exceptional for you to be paid, and standard payments have actually gone down and not up. You have to calculate to what extent it's worth being seen in the magazine before you ask for payment and be prepared for refusal. I used to be paid £75 per page for articles but, these days, I'm as likely to let a magazine in each country have one for free from time to time because it saves paying for advertising

Press releases

A press release is something you may decide to do when you launch a new product tutorial or book or if you are organising an event. Or if you have a newsworthy event which will help you increase brand awareness, such as winning a prize or getting a recommendation from a celebrity or influencer. You need to think about timetabling it and build interest before and after any major press release. Make sure the press release has any necessary links to further information, so that interest that you have whipped up can be acted on immediately.

Magazines and newspapers are often pretty desperate for good content, especially local newspapers. Make sure your press release is eye-catching, informative, concise and easy to rewrite and edit. If you make it easy for them, you're worth more than gold, as they can fill a half page with your brilliant content, or even come back to you for an interview. They just want something that's going to make the readers happy. Be aware that some magazines will expect you to pay for advertising to go along with any feature they do about you. Or they may offer you an advertorial. I don't like these much myself and prefer to have less, but greater quality, exposure. If you know your news is exciting and that the piece is good and well written, you can just play hardball and send a slightly modified version to a competitor if the first paper or magazine won't take it. I have experience of magazine companies who are really nice and some who are pushy. I play nice with the nice ones. We should all be looking for the win-win if we can. If you're a crafter and can write good copy, the craft and design magazines will often get back to you and ask if you will write for them, so make sure you leave the door open for that. It can be the best way to gain a really strong base audience.

Here are the important points to remember for your press release:

Headline: Be sure to make it clear right from the beginning why your story is interesting, important and relevant, but in one single sentence only. This might be difficult to condense and if you can't do it and it's a very important release, hire a copywriter on Fiverr or Upwork, etc. Distilling who and what you are and what the story is about into one sentence is a really useful skill and is worth practising. You can rewrite after you put the text body in. Although a copywriter can only work on what you give them, anyway, as can a journalist.

Description: A few words describing yourself and your company. You should have developed all these ideas after reading the marketing and branding sections. Consider the location. Where are you? Is the news relevant to this location?

Text body: Make sure it's easy to read. You can put the less important material in the second part of this. Do you need quotations or photographs? These can make it easy for a busy journalist to create a good story with the minimum of work. Something visual will catch the attention. It's worth concentrating your mind on how you want the audience to respond to the story. Do you want to increase awareness of your brand? Or maybe you want to invite them to an event or shop. Or is there a never to be repeated offer you want them to be aware of? It's wise to make the story interesting before adding any call to action. Ask yourself. If the call to your shop/website/event were to be taken away would the story stand on its own?

Contact: Include your name, contact details, website and social media links.

> *Top tip: If you're not a good writer yourself, find a copywriter. Even after paying a copywriter you will still be better off than spending on advertising, for much more valuable exposure. If people aren't excited by a story about you, they aren't going to be impressed by your small ads. Give your copywriter your bullet points and let them make magic. But if you want to save money, you can always take a course to learn good copywriting skills yourself*

More free advertising

Writing books about your own work not only brings in royalties but also adds to your kudos in the marketplace. It can also help you sell the materials required if that's part of your business model. For example, I released a book in 2019, the purpose of which was to show an entirely new technique. This new technique pretty much required the buyer to buy our tools. We made it half the price of our normal books both to encourage sales and to signal to our customers that we are aware that we are also selling to them and that we do not wish to profiteer too cynically. There's a fine balance between being a nice person and a businesswoman. I usually err on the side of being nice and this isn't as profitable as it should be! On the other hand, I sleep at night and usually get good reviews. Maybe that means I sell more books etc. A virtuous cycle.

Another form of free advertising is collaborating with other businesses. You may find that there are businesses out there who you befriend, either in real life or on the internet, and your products complement each other. It's not uncommon to be approached and asked if you want to co-promote. Kira dipping in here with an anecdote. One example from my experience is when a digital artist asked if they could make a drawing of one of my products. I agreed, and so they made a beautiful image. When they posted it on Instagram, I quickly gained some more followers. I shared the image via my account, and bagged them some followers, too. Win-win! In some cases, you might even agree to promote and sell both your items together as a bundle.

Paid Advertising

Magazines

In my experience, response rates to almost all small adverts are very low and so it may not be the best method for low value, high volume sales. This is purely my experience, however, and it's certainly possible that I'm wrong. I'm certainly risking the wrath of the craft magazines saying this!

I found very early on, even when distribution figures were much higher, for my business it really didn't pay back. I really didn't have the money anyway. My business was already very visible through the magazines I wrote for. Also, mine was one of the earliest miniatures businesses to have a website back in the mid 1990's. However, I believe that if you work for a very specialist market where people have actually bought the magazine to browse for things to buy (such as wedding magazines), then there may be some value in snaring that high value customer. I would say don't throw money willy nilly at magazine advertising and always keep an eye on the pay back. I've found it to be a dud for me. But that doesn't mean that it won't work for you.

When writing your ads, try to keep them sharp and to the point without too much clutter. Too many advertisers try to cram too much information into the smallest possible space. Honestly, this won't catch anyone's eye and is more likely to put people off. Far from getting more for your money, it could half your ad's impact. The small ads are at the end of a magazine and so, by this time, most readers have flicked through the majority and are now thinking of their next coffee or getting back to work or going into the dentist. Consider the design elements carefully, making sure there is enough empty space around your text for your message to be clear and concise.

In terms of structure, it's likely that you will want your ad to begin with an attention-grabbing headline, have a chunk of text as the "body" which conveys the key benefits of your business and your unique selling points (USPs), and finish with a call to action (CTA). To help prompt ideas, consider why you're writing the ad (i.e. what you want to communicate to the customer and what you want the customer to do with that information), and what might encourage them to act upon seeing it. Finally, don't forget to include your contact details in the ad, or it will all be for nothing! This might include: your website address, your email address, your social media handles, and possibly your telephone number.

Digital paid advertising

There are loads of videos on the subject of paid digital ads. I have very little to add to these experienced advertisers. I'm not sure they work as well for small businesses as they do for larger companies. They take a significant investment in money, time or both to refine your promotions, but I will share my personal experience.

One thing to note is to make sure you're targeting the right audience with your ads. You don't want your ads shown to people who aren't likely to buy your products. For example, you don't want to be advertising to the very elderly or young children if you are Countess Bascula with your rather lovely boned corsets, for example. Of course, if you do advertise to them, these people may

well click on those ads just out of curiosity. And you will have to pay for those clicks, whether or not they result in a sale.

Facebook ads

In order to try Facebook ads, my advice is to wait until they have a voucher offer. Match it with a little money of your own and find your way around the targeting by simply doing it. It's cheap practise in targeting. Facebook ads produced much less than I was hoping for. I did produce two ads, but the reach seemed to be lower than they appeared to be offering. I wasn't impressed and, as far as I know, for a spend of 30 euros I got precisely no feedback. This is only a personal opinion, but I think your money could currently be better spent. I'd be prepared to try again in a year to see if anything has improved but at the moment I feel you can get better reach just by providing interesting content.

I don't think Facebook has cottoned on fully to the needs of micro businesses. But as they themselves say, they move fast and break things, so they could soon realise that if they provided a simpler and cheaper method for micro businesses to get real results, they would have a ready market. After all, most of us use their platform.

Pinterest ads

I had better apparent reach results with Pinterest, but I spent around 30 euros and got a couple of Pinterest repins. Once again, the reports appear a little strange. The number of reported clicks on the Pinterest advertising performance analytics did not appear to tally with our own reports of traffic to our website and reported only one visit through Pinterest. I was charged for a couple of dozen. Once again, I'll leave that until enough time has passed for me to understand it better, or if they improve the service and the reporting. I did have a hiccup at first which told me that I was only reaching Spain. I had to reset that, or rather, get my husband to reset it for me.

Amazon Ads

As an Amazon seller, you can get Amazon to promote your items as a sponsored ad alongside other people's goods, either in the first page or underneath as suggestions. Take a look next time you're shopping on Amazon. Watch how they put other similar or related items under your nose. For example, if you know someone else is selling an item similar to yours you can target their product specifically for your advertising using their product descriptions or even their product ASIN number

(Amazon's unique product identifier, like an ISBN). Or you can target specific keywords such as "wedding cake topper". You can also catch any similar phrase like "wedding topper", which might have your product shown to someone looking for top hats. This could be OK, because the person who wants the hat may think "Ooh, I want one of those!" and possibly even buy it. Or they might just click out of nosiness and never buy. Cost to you 30 cents and sale value, nothing. So, you might want to filter them out in favour of "exact phrase only". Or you could instead agree to pay two cents for that click which might result in a sale. Then you can adjust your bid for better placements on the page or better times of day for better customers. Amazon doesn't give you all its secrets; it simply calls this "dynamic bidding", which means you can choose to follow their advice and almost literally gamble extra that the people they think are more likely to buy really do become customers.

I have had some success with their book advertising so I give this one a cautious thumbs up.

You can find instructional videos on YouTube to help you with this complicated subject but if you decide to try it you are going to have to set aside some time and a budget and be prepared to make a few mistakes. If you're selling books, I recommend Dave Chesson's videos. Remember, Amazon is always changing things and you may think you understand the path through targeting only to find when you get there, that things have changed.

Google Ads (formerly Google Adwords)

We don't personally have any experience of using Google Ads, but apparently it can be good for use by small businesses as well as larger ones. If you're interested in checking it out, here's a nice clear tutorial on YouTube:

https://www.youtube.com/ watch?v=WmepvHQOHXg

If you feel that it's worth having a marketing campaign on Google or Amazon but you want to concentrate on production, hiring agencies to manage your Pay Per Click and paid search might be worth doing.

Whatever you decide to do with digital advertising, make sure you keep a close eye on what does and doesn't convert into sales. Nobody wants to throw money down the drain. And remember, all of this is my advice only. I'd suggest that you don't take too much notice of suggested bids unless it's to steer you away from the expensive bids and towards a mine of undiscovered relevance. That is to say, when targeting keywords or products, you're looking for relationships between goods people are buying and your goods. You want to find the keyword and product relationships that other sellers haven't found, and bid for those. It can be a fun game if you have time and money to spend.

Hiring paid marketing and advertising management

If you have no time to spend but you do want to rapidly increase your sales of items that are easily repeatable with the minimum of your hands-on time, then hiring help with marketing and paid ads could be the right option for you. There are many virtual business assistants easily accessible online, and the recent pandemic has produced even more. Upwork is a good source of these. There are also lots of Facebook business networking groups with all levels of business support services. If parts of this book are too much to cope with, you can have your very small business function more like a much bigger business simply by deciding what you can outsource that you don't have time to take on yourself.

If you want more control and knowledge, you can get a business mentorship package. These can start very cheaply and can go into the hundreds and thousands. Some are really worth having and some are just rehashes of knowledge you can get on YouTube. You can get a lot of what you need for free, but where mentorship helps is with self-discipline. They take you through the process step-by-step until you too can speak corporate marketing jargon with the best of them (if that's what floats your boat). Find someone whose advice resonates with you in the free presentations.

Don't get taken in by the big sell straight away. Someone's work might be worth hundreds or thousands, but equally there are some pretty slick marketing funnels out there. If this is the first time you've read the term "marketing funnel", don't worry. You'll hear it a lot when you go looking for marketing advice. It's just used to describe the process of turning someone from a viewer to a customer. Usually with some kind of click-bait. Like, "Would you like to know how to keep your craft room organised?". I can almost hear you shouting "Hell yes!", so I'm sure you can imagine how many clicks that would get from crafters. Then, the object is to squeeze them down the "funnel". That is to say, to get them to take the next step. So next might be a free download on clearing and storing ideas, and after that it might be "Buy our special crafter storage solutions course". As you may be able to tell from my tone, I have a somewhat negative attitude to the heavy-handed sales pitch. The truth is; however, most mentors and agencies use them. They do work. And they will work on you, so you have to be aware of the process to have your careful buyer head on when buying mentorship packages. You may even find yourself convinced to use those tactics yourself!

Measuring your own marketing performance

As well as having a marketing strategy you also need a process of evaluating that strategy, so give yourself a periodic review, even if you're a sole trader. If you have set a timetable by which you wish to achieve certain marketing goals, you also need to set a timetable to evaluate which of those goals and strategies have made a difference to your business, and which are a waste of your time. Keep an eye on any analytics which are available to you, and keep figures of rising and falling sales after various marketing campaigns.

Make charts if you can with details of how much time or money you have invested and what your return has been. They don't have to be 100% accurate for you to get a feel for what is working, what you might need to add and what strategies you need to cut. For example, if you are spending four hours a week putting pictures on Instagram, but nobody is being driven to your site, then it may be time to keep it as a one-post-per-week

platform. Or perhaps you need to examine why your calls-to-action might not be converting social media viewers into customers and potentially change the type of post you're making.

The quickest and most accurate way to gather data on your online performance is by using free Google Analytics tools, which we touched on in the "Keywords" section. It's a great way to monitor the traffic to your website and provides you with lots of valuable insights on where your visitors are coming from, who they are, how they find you and, importantly, how many visitors convert into buyers.

You can also connect your GA (Google Analytics) account to your social media accounts, which will really help monitor your online marketing efforts, showing you what is and isn't working in detail. GA gathers all this data and automatically creates charts and graphs to make the information easy to understand. It even highlights errors on your site which you might not have otherwise noticed, such as redirect errors, allowing you to fix them as and when required. There are plenty of great resources online that can explain how to use Google Analytics in more detail, however, my advice is simply to get started with making an account and learn as you go along!

Takeaway: *Monitoring your marketing performance allows you to see what's working and what isn't, as well as how your customers behave. This helps you to improve as you go along, giving you vital clues on what your customers want and how to cater to them.*

15. When trouble hits

Consciously problem-solving

There are two basic ways of thinking. We all do both of these at times in our lives. The reason why some people seem mellow and yet also energetic is because they hop off the first way of thinking on to the second more often. Here's the first way of thinking:

"Things happen to me."

We all have friends or friends on social media where it becomes even more obvious which level of thinking they are currently on because you only have their words to read from. These are the people who appear to have the attitude when coming across a problem "what-s the worst that can happen - I'm sure it will happen to me". And you will often read posts which contain the acronym FML (F*** My Life). This is the more severe end of "things happen to me" thinking and we can all slip into it from time to time. My dad was a "things happen to me" thinker most of the time, with occasional bouts of making things happen.

The other is:

"I make things happen."

The other type of friend at the other end seems like a whirlwind. Constantly positive, constantly cheerful. Constantly achieving, sometimes to an exhausting extent. My mum was one of these, with occasional bouts of tiredness.

They were both creative and both hard workers. One of them was almost always happy with their lot. The other was almost always worried about the next thing that might go wrong. My parents were fairly extreme in their difference but not totally so, because they had each other as a balance. Do you know which type you are? You might need this self-knowledge later.

In this kind of couple, the one simply has to trust the other from time to time. I probably channelled my mother more to be honest. There were times of anxiety where I worried I'd made the wrong decisions. But whenever I knew what I wanted to achieve in the end, I worked out a path based on "I make things happen." And they always did. People, therefore, think I'm always an outgoing confident person. The truth is nearer to that I have both personalities as do most of us. I simply choose to channel the one that's most exciting to me in my work life. The one that I've learned gets results. Then I'll go back into my shell from time to time to take a break.

When making big life decisions you simply have to decide which of these sides of yourself to channel. The cautious, problem-avoiding one, or the making-things-happen one. Yes, there will be problems with the second. In the second scenario though, the problems are almost always not as big as you fear and you will, with courage, achieve more.

Sometimes these personality types are over-simplified into can't-do and can-do mentality. But you can overcome "impostor syndrome" and self-doubt.

Googling how to solve a problem can certainly help, but I do believe in discussion either with yourself or with others, too. Asking friends and community members can give you other points of view. If you go to Google with a negative or misguided perspective, you could receive confirmation bias if you see a complicated result. Do bear in mind that your friends will also be biased too, or just telling you what they know you want to hear. The point is to try different avenues to solve your problems and stay open-minded.

First of all, you need to identify the problem and then you may need to mind map it. Look at all the possible doors and all the possible windows. Maybe even sleep on it. In fact there are very few problems that don't have some kind of solution. The trick is to find the ones worth solving, and let the other ones go.

Often the solution to your problem is simply to spend a set amount of time, maybe a day or even a week learning how to do something new, or developing a new product by experimentation.

Takeaway: Whenever you have a really good idea, note it down. Look at where it fits in your current scheme. Weigh up its relevance and add it to your plan as a for later if it can't be done now. You can always look back at it when your head is clearer and solve the problems then. There is always a solution.

Artists' block

"What can I do when I don't feel like creating? Or when I'm certain that I've finally run out of ideas?"

We all have days, weeks or months when we have a little or a lot of artists' block. I think this is often down to mental health. All of us, to a greater or lesser extent, have ebbs and flows in our "mojo". Some of my patrons have a greater degree of highs and lows. This seems to be a pretty common trait among artists and when we are "up" we find ourselves super creative, but we can have matching downs when the inspiration simply doesn't flow. Just like most psychological problems I feel we really need to embrace these ups and downs and work through them, doing the donkey work while inspiration is low and doing the creative work while it's high. But what happens when we've gotten stuck on low? Or when we have a deadline to get something done and we really need to kick-start something?

Although there is some validity in the "just do it" philosophy that you should just pick up the clay or the glass, the chisel or the pen and simply get started on something, that leaves out all the very real physical and mental reasons why you might just not be firing on all your cylinders.

Well, there are some ways to recharge the batteries physically. We can rest and get better sleep. We can take up walking or running, or yoga and meditation. At least one of my Patrons is a runner, with a keen interest in how it can help your mental health. And from her experiences and those of her friends, it works. Personally, I'm more of a walker. But, whatever your preferred form of exercise, I know for a fact that when I push myself up to my limit a few times, my energy, both physical and mental, improves. Of course, it goes without saying that improved blood flow improves your mental function and yet us crafters sit for long periods for days on end doing precious little but crafting, and this is bound to affect our long term physical and mental health.

Others among us have had family issues to cope with. The ill health of others, family disagreements, workplace stress, bereavements, and financial worries can all contribute to negative feelings and not only an inability to "get started" on anything, but also a lack of drive to do so. When we've had this for an extended period of time, it becomes self-fulfilling. We're afraid of the block...and

that blocks us. So it's also important to deal with the fear of failure.

Angie's 5 point plan for starting to push through the block:

1. Take some exercise, and some B vitamins (for your nervous system health). Breathe in and, more importantly, breathe out. You can't get more in if you don't let some go. That's true in many areas of your life! When you're tense, you hold things in. When you're relaxed, you let them go.

2. Buy a new tool or try a new technique. When I first got a new laptop I spent the first 24 hours unable to open it because I simply didn't know where to start. But it was a new tool for me. Once I got over that issue, it caused its own inspiration and gave rise to this book. It's a matter of your mindset. Instead of thinking about how big and new and scary the concept is, think "what can I do with this tool that I couldn't do before?". For me, it was a matter of getting ideas down instantly, as soon as they occurred to me. In bed, on the sofa, on trips. Before, I'd scribbled ideas in books and then never looked at them again. I had loads of ideas. My plan was to share them on Patreon. But because there was no easy way to record them, the scribbles never got typed up and uploaded. So, what had been a great idea for sharing inspiration, simply became a chore. I don't have that excuse now. So, to break my 24 hour blank on how to use my laptop, I took it to bed and, as soon as I woke up, I put it on my knee and wrote down my first thoughts of the day. I was away! And now I can't stop. Your new tool or toy may be a book of new techniques, may be a new and better sewing machine or some moulds or a new brand of clay. Whatever it is, follow this approach to finding out what you can do with it that you couldn't do before and you'll take the first tentative steps which will break the invisible handcuffs on you.

3. Get rid of fear of failure. Embrace it. Failure is an option. In fact, failure is a prerequisite for new ideas. It's very rare anyone does anything right that they haven't done wrong first, or someone else hasn't done wrong first and passed on the solution for. If you're trying to come up with a new idea that's all, or even partly, your own, you are going to make mistakes. Lots of them. Some of them small and the occasional humongous ones. Learn to pat yourself on the back for learning something instead of beating yourself up for getting it wrong. That's how you invent things. And I'll let you in on another little secret. You can ignore people that tell you something

can't be done and you can try to do it anyway. Unless, of course, it's obviously dangerous. I'm always being told, "you can't", and that's when I get excited. Because maybe I can! And because I'm hard-headed, often I do. A barrier is just an invitation to look at a problem from another angle.

4. If your mental block is about how to move your creative business forward, you almost definitely need to do some reading to wake up your creative brain. Connect with a new Facebook group or examine some Pinterest boards or take a Skillshare class to help reinspire you.

5. Then there's the "just get on with it" mantra. Put times and dates in your diary when you're going to go into your creating space and just start. Give yourself a goal and don't worry any further about whether you'll achieve your goal. The starting is the hardest bit. Honestly!

Takeaway: *Relax. Artists' block is normal. Don't fear it. Take a few days off but set a date to sit yourself down and produce something. Allow other people or places to inspire you. Ask someone whether they want to give you a creative challenge. Once the ball gets rolling again; you'll be fine.*

Try a 100 day challenge to trigger and hone your creativity

What is a 100 day challenge? Why should you consider doing one and, more importantly, what could taking one on do for your business? After all, you're already short of time, often feeling pushed to the very limit.

Most creators thrive in the area of problem-solving and the way we solve them is the mark of our unique styles. Those of us who are in "proper" tax paying businesses, however, can often get stuck in the day to day business of earning a living. Because of that we can fail to develop our art. We can even fall behind our friends who don't have the constraints of earning a living to consider and can dedicate more time to perfecting theirs.

The creative mind functions like a muscle. The more it's exercised the more capable it is, and sometimes we drown it under practicalities. That in itself can hold your business back while the competition thrives. The idea of setting yourself a fairly rigorous challenge is to allow yourself that creative exercise and to push yourself beyond your current boundaries and mental blocks. You allow yourself back into that childlike, wondrous state of thinking "what happens if I...". This enables you to give yourself problems to solve and, solving them gives your inspiration and energy a new boost.

I always did like a challenge. So why not 100 of them? I began thinking about how bountiful nature is and, more exactly, how many flowers I would need to learn to make if I was going to pursue the new market for my miniatures that I'd had my eye on.

In my case, a few months ago I decided to take a serious look at the wedding market. Not, you might think, an obvious market for a miniaturist, but think again. For example, what would you prefer to give or receive as a bridal favour? A little something you will probably throw away, or a real 12th scale miniature item? Even non-miniaturists are smitten by small things and unlikely to throw them away. They will be passed on if they aren't wanted. At the higher end, bridal favours could well come into the miniatures bracket. Of course, more brides are now making their own crafty gifts and that would be my area too - to supply the tools. I really would like to have a go at making 12th scale replicas of bridal bouquets. So the idea of making 50 new flowers and 50 new leaves or plant stencils popped into my head.

I have to say that challenge was quite an experience! It had some unexpected consequences too. I've already changed the way I do several things for the better. Also, I now have enough new designs to keep us going for several months, or even years if released only a few at a time. I'm now working at the absolute limits of our tool making abilities and my own eyesight. I've tried using tools I've always wondered about. I also came up with designs I never thought possible, because the problems have to have solutions so I found them. As if that weren't a good enough reason to do it, meanwhile I was keeping my Patreon subscribers entertained by sharing those day to day innovations.

Another benefit is that my husband and I started to communicate designs more effectively through repetitive practice. This means our design process is streamlined, and he's learned more about how nature works. We've come up with better versions of several of our current stencils. I got several really good ideas for additional products, including Christmas baubles with my plants and flower bunches in too. I enjoyed the process so much that I had my next challenge ready before I'd finished. This, of course, is tied up with the next book I want to write. Working smart means if I can kill two birds with one stone, I will. I can write up the challenge ideas as

I make things. After that, I'd like to learn and practice illustration over 100 days.

Maybe yours could be a challenge to learn a new skill which will take you past a problem you're experiencing. For example, I could have chosen as my task simply watching one video on flower arranging every day for a week. Actually, I did some of that too. If you set yourself the correct tasks, you might find that your time is even more productive since you'll be working smarter and with renewed enthusiasm. If you're already overburdened, make sure any new things you innovate are priced at a higher level to give you more time to make better work. This can be the start of a virtuous cycle. If your time is really short, make your challenge fit your needs. It could be just one 10 minute sketch a day in a 100 page journal. And remember, it doesn't have to be good!

Overwhelm

"I can't cope and can't seem to get anything done even though I'm busier than ever!"

Artists aren't always good business people - we tend to be more creative than business minded. I think most of us know that deep down. Those who are, are very lucky indeed. If you're not, however, don't beat yourself up about this, because maybe you were dealt a hand that contained more innovation than organisational ability. This isn't to say a business-leaning artist can't develop their creative innovation and neither does it mean an innovative artist cannot develop some business sense. But it takes some effort and often it's effort we don't think we have time to put in because we're way too busy with our creative flow.

But there are times you need to stand back and take stock rather than collapse with exhaustion. Those times can come out of the blue with the "straw that broke the camel's back". We may not even realise that we are getting overwhelmed. We may be enjoying the pressure of working to deadlines, pulling 7 day weeks and burning the midnight oil before a fair until that last little thing arrives. Maybe it's a tax bill or a family crisis. It doesn't matter what causes it. You suddenly feel like you can't cope and you just want to disappear and not answer the phone or the door. You may be sleeping badly and worrying about the things you've avoided. Whether or not your business is a sideline or a full time tax paying business, you need a plan. And to make a plan you need to know what it is about your business that you love and what you hate. You need to learn to say no to some of the people who are demanding your time and you need to get back to basics. If any of this resonates with you, you need to take a deep breath and a notepad and a cuppa. Close the business for a day or two and make time to breathe.

I've thoroughly overdone it to get that last piece done or to make more of an item that I think might be popular, only to find that this isn't the item that sells. If you're hitting the wall just before a fair or event, ask yourself

what you can manage without. What difference it would really make if you didn't get that last thing done, compared with what difference it would make if you were ill and couldn't go or couldn't function when you got there. You may need to put off the full on self-examination until after the event, but stop pushing yourself too hard now and get some meditative packing done. That last piece of work may not get done but you'll have all your needs with you at the fair instead of forgetting something vital in the rush to make just one more handbag. Everything will be well packed and labelled. Then you won't feel frazzled at the event. That's one thing you can do to take the weight off and to stop burnout in its tracks.

So. You're home, you've realised you're in trouble and that everything's getting too much and that your panic means you aren't functioning properly. Put aside the immediate. Grab a decaffeinated drink. Get away from the screen. Get your pen and paper. First of all, you can just write down the things that are worrying you. The obvious things like the bills first. The not-so-obvious things like the things you feel. Maybe you feel you're letting your family down. Maybe you feel you aren't doing your best work because you're too rushed. You worry your client will hate it, and nobody will ever buy from you again. Write all this down no matter how implausible. Just write. It may be painful, but it's like the confessional. You can't forgive yourself until you know what's wrong. And you can't know what's wrong if you're too busy plate spinning to take stock.

You might start off thinking it's all about the bills or missing your daughter's concert, the row you had with your partner, or a missing parcel. You could end up realising that those things are just symptoms of the fact that you've lost your feeling of control or direction over your business, or even over your art itself.

So write down the argument you had with a customer and how unreasonable you thought they were and maybe the little hidden regret that you could have handled it another way. Write down how much you hate doing the books, or the emails, or the sanding down, or the packaging. Write down the things that you're avoiding because they're the bits that you hate. And now write down which are the parts of the business that you love. What would you walk over hot coals to keep doing? If you can, write down what it is that keeps you crafting. For me, it's the fact that I love to invent simple solutions to problems. What is your "I really love to…"? If you are so overwhelmed, open your mind to the possibility that you might need to change something.

After all that catharsis you should go for a long walk or take a hot bath or do the washing up that you've let pile up. Anything that gives you time to empty your mind. Then start to forgive yourself for not being perfect.

Now call or email that customer and apologise for being late. Tell them you'd got a bit overwhelmed and give them a new date for delivery and make that new date far enough away to leave you a full week of not working on it. But also give them the option to cancel the order and refund the money. You may need to cancel a fair or at least allow yourself to be a bit more relaxed about it. You may need to apply for time to get your tax declaration in, if that's possible or ask to get the payment delayed. This is possible although it may cost more.

Ask yourself if all that sounds very unlike you, or even seems impossible. What's the worst that can happen if you do that? And what's the worst if you don't? Sometimes the problem makes you fear the solution. Especially if that solution is a simple apology. If you're heading for burnout, it will be obvious what you need to do. This may be exactly what you are avoiding. Do those things one by one. The people who you might think are causing you this distress may be your solution.

Life is full of negatives and stuff or people that seem to want to bar your way. The trick is to be the kind of person who likes the challenge of a closed door and the trip around it.

Now you want to rebuild your business in a different way. With a different focus. You may need to go back to your scribbles. Look back at the goal setting. The "your life balance" game at the beginning of the book. You may find it better just to turn over a new leaf. Do you remember the parts of the business that you love? Write them down again. And on the opposite page the parts that you hate.

Are you a sole trader and there's nobody else in the business? Or do you have a partner who also works in the business? Or a business partner (two different things of course)? If you're a sole trader, you don't have to consult anyone else about the future of your business or how you spend your time over the next few days and weeks If you are in any kind of a partnership you may have to ask for time out. And for meetings along the way to talk about new strategies. But even if you're completely alone, you'll still need to take time asking yourself what will really work for you.

If there are parts of the business that you realise you really hate, ask yourself if there's a way you can negotiate passing that job to your partner or employing someone to do it. I think, for example, hating doing the books is fairly common. Currently, my husband runs the business end of the business, so I get to pass that task on (lucky me). He hates it too. But not as much as we hated paying 80 euros a month out to our accountant. Actually, if we could have afforded it, we would happily have paid that out, but that was one thing we had to take on when our business was in crisis. You have to decide on the balance of some of these divisions of labour. On balance, I couldn't function while worrying about the books.

If you're a solopreneur and don't have a partner who can help with your business, can you afford to have someone take this worry off your shoulders, at least until you get the rest sorted out? If you can…do. The first step is to identify the most easy to solve problems and find ways of taking those off your overall load.

Sometimes the solutions are right under your nose, but because you've never written the problems down you haven't given yourself time to solve them. For example, I was overwhelmed in part because my house was a mess, my cats were shedding, and I was getting asthma and allergy attacks. Because I was so overwhelmed with the rest of my business, I wasn't getting the housework done, plus my dishwasher had broken and I couldn't afford a new one. I used to get a cleaner to come from time to time. The problem was she spent half her time smoking and chatting on the phone. Despite the fact that I didn't pay her in money, but in an hour of my time teaching English. To be honest, she was still too expensive! This was getting me down and affecting my work. The solution was quite simple. I bought an air purifier and a robot vac instead of upgrading my dishwasher. I now wash up by hand. My vacuum cleaner tinkers around the house all the while making sure that my cats slink off and curl up while it deals with the dust and fluff. This gives me meditation time. The added bonus is the pleasure I get from calling this robot names when the stupid thing finds a place to get stuck. I could never do that with the cleaning lady! Another useful effect is that I have to be a bit tidier because otherwise the robot gets "amorous" with any tools and equipment left on the floor. Your problem will be a different one. But there's always a solution if you give yourself some space and time to think laterally.

Sometimes you're overwhelmed because of a sudden burst of success

This is where you have to look again at your 5-year plan and your cash flow forecasts. Are you on your own or do you have a partner/partners in the business? Do you have anybody who is already working with you part time who could become full time? And how do you feel about being an employer or a contractor? How do you feel about stepping back from the craft and starting to do more managing? Also, how do you feel about potentially taking on debt to invest in the business? For some people this is easy and for some it's simply not an option. Think about delegating tasks to business agencies. Think again about Upwork or PeoplePerHour.

Sometimes the overwhelm comes from a change in personal circumstances

Unexpected changes in personal circumstances such as a change in your own health, wellbeing or finances, or those of a family member, can really throw a spanner in the works. It could mean re-thinking your initial strategy. In the last few years, I've stepped back more and more from the production side of my business. This is because we needed to grow and make more income but, perversely, I needed to do less making. This is because making is very time-intensive and low on profit. After an unexpected health scare of mine, we decided to invest (very heavily for us) in a laser cutting machine that Frank could use. This was initially to make papercraft packs for miniaturists but became much more important as it gave me time to step back from the work I had been doing, giving me more time to be inventive. That time for inventiveness led me to a whole new technique that I could write about, teach and sell tools and materials for. What seems like a negative change can easily turn into positive decisions. Make sure you only work where you are most effective, particularly when you're dealing with difficult circumstances. The recent COVID-19 pandemic had a similar effect on the creative world. For better or worse, many people looked much harder at their needs and decided that they needed less work...or indeed more. Many were fortunate enough to be able to use the time to learn new skills and to make new plans. Some of those people might even be reading this book right now!

Strategy meetings

What a difference having strategy meetings has made to our business over the last year! We've been struggling to get organised for years because we both have lazy moments and hard working moments, and because we're both self employed and not ruled by the clock, we also suffered from an unhealthy level of procrastination. So we decided we needed not only some self-discipline but also to help each other with a bit of accountability.

These can be pretty informal affairs and tend to revolve around a large creamy coffee and maybe something tasty to eat. If you're just a one-person business, have the meeting with yourself. It's all about settings aside some time to think about the future, creating goals and an action plan.

"But I'm on my own. I can't have a meeting with myself!"

Of course you can! You can sit and allow the creative and the business side of yourself to connect. Just schedule 10 minutes each day with a notebook or a calendar such as Google Calendar and simply fill in your short term and long term goals and look through what you've written before. Have you done any of those? Tick them off if you have. Have any changed their urgency level? Re-prioritise them if so. Are there any long-term dreams or fantasies you want to work towards? Write them down. Decide on today's tasks. Finish your coffee and you'll be more ready to get down to it. Some people like to start the day with a personal affirmation. Mine used to be "healthy, happy, loving, and kind". That was all very well for my mental health. But I have a new one for my business mind. Smart, creative and successful. It doesn't hurt to give my business ego a boost from time to time.

Batch production

Taking on too many commissions or too many events can cause you to feel overwhelmed. Divide your calendar up and stop working towards the next fair. This sounds counterintuitive, but don't make work for the next fair until two weeks before the fair. Work instead for the next-but-one. Batch-make things even if you are an OOAK (one of a kind) worker. There's no point in making just one bow for a corset, one pair of teddy bear shoes, or single individual parts for one item that you make a lot of. You can recombine batch-made items into further pieces in the series or save them until later. One thing I've found is that it's uncomfortable to go back and make something again because you need just one. It can be fun making a dozen of the same thing all at once but not over and over. So ride the wave of your own interest until it's totally spent. This will make you more productive in the long term, increasing your profits. If you make ten of the same thing and then suddenly find a better way of doing it, which looks more beautiful, and you find yourself hating your earlier work, nothing is lost. You have a few options here. One is fixed: don't keep substandard work when you have reached a higher quality. Sell it off in a cheap bin or, better still, give it away

to children, or others, who will be enchanted! Don't think of this as a loss, think of it as a double gain. The first is that you have honed your skill, and are now much improved for it. The second is that you have inspired another person who may perhaps be your future customer or a maker themselves, since in some way you have added to the sum of their inspiration.

I nearly forgot this top stress busting tip. I'm a bit of a live-to-work-er. My husband and business partner is a bit of a work-to-live-er. I absolutely do admire that personality and I need more of that laid-back attitude in my life. Except for one thing. Everything becomes stressful when it's last minute. This one thing is so important for combatting stress that it's almost a mantra at home and it's this: "stock on shelves!". This means you should take the article you have sold OFF the site until you have made or ordered more of them. I know that in the resale world, just-in-time stock systems work well. For the craft business, though, advertising something that isn't in stock is an absolute no-no, even if you find it relatively easy to make. You end up messing about trying to find the parts and materials to make just one item at a time, making the customer wait. This behaviour eats time, and it eats away at customer satisfaction.

Takeaway: Exercise will clear away the cobwebs. Invest sensibly in what you need to help you stay on track. Self-discipline, routine and structure will help you to undo the negative pressures and create step-by-step solutions to your immediate problems, rebuilding confidence in your problem solving ability.

16. Getting through to retirement:
The artist's pension plan

Let's face it; I don't know any artists who have a pension plan. Do you? Life is already too uncertain, and income often too meagre to make grand plans. At least we could never put money into some scheme which could later "disappear". One day, however, we hit that wall of realisation as I did on the last days of my 50s where even the tiny state pension didn't arrive because of new pension rules.

This section is useful to those who are already in business and are struggling, especially if you're looking forward and only seeing poverty for your years of being creative. It will also help new business owners, or those who are thinking of starting a business, protect against the ups and downs of life and gain a sense of relaxed control.

Most people are looking forward to that magic day when you can stop working and travel the world or look after a tiny allotment or sit at street cafes with your friends putting the world to rights. Whatever your political persuasion or beliefs on the subject of income and pensions, it looks like this isn't going to happen for most of us, and we're all going to work until we drop. Because we are the people who are less shocked by this prospect. Who are less afraid of a sudden loss of income since we face it every day. But we shouldn't be too complacent because a life without any money can be cruel, especially when you're older. So here are a few ideas to look at while there is still time or even at the 11th hour. I hit this wall 3 years ago when, just half a year off my 60th birthday, I was diagnosed with a potentially terminal disease. Both my husband and myself were running our miniatures business where I was the maker and he was all the admin, and the person who dealt with the website and optimised all my photos into beautiful images and posted on social media for me as well as laying out my books such as they were at the time. Neither of us were very organised and our income was already pitifully low when our bombshell hit. That was a difficult year. But where the illness was a terrible blow, I can now say it was also a gift because it gave me time and the need to re-evaluate our life plans. We had absolutely nothing... or so I thought.

But then I realised I had the tools to help myself. We both already had the tools to help ourselves. I had the knowledge from 3 decades in the business that people wanted. I had shelves full of partially complete projects. Many of them were actually in forgotten places in my computer filing system. These projects and writings had a value that my need motivated me to release. I realised every mistake I'd ever made, every single "daft idea" I'd ever had, had a future use. They were like diamonds to be mined, albeit compacted under layers of self-doubt and frustration. So here was my pension pot. Not under the mattress or in the bank. Not in pounds or euros or stocks and bonds, but in easily mined jewels of information. So that's what we started doing. My advice for those of you who are just starting out, is to write down everything you do. The formula for every glue or colour or idea you invent, because this could be part of your pension pot too. Not just if you're older; it's always worth looking at what you have got and what other ways there are to monetise it. And here they are. The other ways I made my work pay. The reason we've climbed out of having nothing, and my five year plan is now bearing fruit.

Moving to multiple income streams, repeating business and passive income for a more secure future

So how can you guarantee yourself more per hour? Simply raising the price of your work is tricky in your first year of business, especially if you've already set your prices at "I need the money" levels. The best answer is to find extra channels of income which work for you alongside your crafting. This is known as creating multiple income streams; adding together several small incomes to create a more comfortable one. There are lots of ways to do this, many of which I've tried (particularly in the last 3 years since the start of my new 5 year plan).

Since my own illness where my income dropped through the floor, I came to several realisations. One was that I had a great deal of work and a great deal of knowledge that I had not been business savvy enough to "monetise". If you've never heard that word before or have heard it, but aren't sure what it means, it basically means finding ways of making your day to day work and communications pay. It's generally used to refer to all those activities that don't produce a physical output but do have a value. So, for example, you may have decided to show all your fans how you made that beautiful sausage dog pendant. Or you may have written a tutorial...or both. Monetising is making sure (usually by some form of micropayment) that you're paid for your time and effort. This is how YouTubers get paid. Not much, unless they go viral, but some do. But these are some of the ways you can improve that income.

Often, multiple income streams are referred to as "passive income" because, once you have created the product, you sit back and let the money come in. This makes it sound like lazy business but it isn't. You simply invest time and effort upfront into making a product that's repeatable without any further effort on your part. This is expensive in time upfront but pays out more over the longer term. This smooths out your income and also allows you to cash in your lifelong learning if you are an older more experienced artist. It's a new way of doing business which happens to particularly lend itself to older artists. Well, we have to get something for those years of unpaid slog!

Several of the following now form a part of my multiple income stream. They may get you thinking about your business strategy, and we'll discuss them in a little more detail next.

Potential income streams list:

*   *Craft classes at home*
*   *Private craft classes in students' home*
*   *Art prints, T shirts, fabric design*
*   *Reproductions*
*   *Video (YouTube, vlogging etc)*
*   *Book royalties*
*   *Mentoring and teaching on subscription platforms*
*   *Podcasting*
*   *Selling PDFs of patterns*
*   *Selling SVGs for laser cutters or plotter cutter machine users*
*   *Private mentoring or teaching*
*   *Patreon*
*   *Ko-fi*
*   *Crowdfunding such as Kickstarter, GoFundMe and Venmo*

Put "side hustles" into your browser and see what comes up in the search results. There were a good few I hadn't thought of.

Making your work pay more than once

This is especially relevant if you don't want to make a thousand of the same style of sausage dogs or what have you, no matter how beautiful they are. If you're motivated more by a desire to move on and invent something else, these are some of the ways you can use your existing inventions, photographs and writing to leverage a greater number of incomes across several platforms.

Most high-flyers in industry are earning the wages they do because they are profitable to their bosses. They make assets that are worth more than their hourly wage. You and your abilities are a saleable asset. People want to see what you do next. They want to own one of your pieces of work, read one of your books. If you have lots of ideas for beautiful and saleable products it's certainly worth looking at investing time in your easily duplicated assets rather than letting the professional copyists duplicate them and take the income from your intellectual property.

Let's look at the easiest options first.

Print on demand merchandise

Firstly, photographs of your work can be printed on ancillary items.

Painters can have their work sold as high quality prints See

http://www.nickystevensongallery.com

for examples of my new favourite artist's limited edition prints. Would your work reproduce as high quality prints or greetings cards or postcards? There are other ways to reproduce items as a limited edition alongside your one of a kind pieces. Try Redbubble which costs nothing and is easy to upload to and which prints on a huge range of items. Redbubble seems to be worldwide and I'm currently testing it myself with a range of miniaturist specific greetings cards and some of my other work. The great thing about these platforms is that you can reuse your work for a completely different purpose or to support and advertise your main business. We're even going to try it out with our Countess Bascula character from this book. I'm told Americans tend to use Zazzle. Or Wraptious is a similar company serving the UK. You can even have your designs printed onto fabric with companies like Spoonflower. All simply custom-print to order and advertise your products as part of their extensive range of artists' work. Wraptious started recruiting a very small number of artists through competitions but is expanding to take in a broader range of artists. You can even just use these companies as a market testing tool.

Anything that flies on those, you could then get printed in greater numbers and take to market yourself. I just asked for a quote from UK printing company OutFox and to get 100 greetings cards printed costs around 75 pounds (around 100 dollars). A big outlay for an untested product but a very small outlay for a tested one.

Another friend of mine puts his quirky and sometimes rather rude ideas on T shirts and mugs at home, **https://www.clemwear.com** using simple easily obtained equipment. I think he proves that you don't have to be a 'fine artist' to be creative and to sell repeatable work that makes people happy and amused.

If you make sculptural products, have you thought of limited edition reproductions? Caroline McFarlane Watts, a Brit who now lives and works in California, is owner of Tall Tales Productions

https://www.tall-tales.com She produces delightful characters both for the animation industry and for sale. She now produces limited editions of her work as collectible items. I suppose that they are cast in resin. They are still limited edition and are still wonderful art pieces to own but she spreads the cost of her art over a number of collectors. Take a look at how delightful they are and ask yourself who wouldn't want to own one, even though they aren't one of a kind.

Tutorials

Tutorials (aka how-to videos), are a great way to increase your following and get people interested in your work. You have to have a bit of a thick skin about copying, but that's easy if you aren't too precious about your work and you do like inspiring others. If every time you made a new product you took photographs or video and wrote up how you did it, it might take you a little longer, but you could be investing time now into a more passive income down the line. You can publish on YouTube but the income is very small. Other options include Skillshare, Teachable, Udemy or even a private subscription Facebook group. All of these are more profitable than YouTube if you can get the students. On the other hand, one viral YouTube video will supercharge the whole of your business. There's no reason at all why you can't do both and drive people from YouTube to your more profitable private classes. Also bear in mind that, just like when writing product descriptions for the internet, video descriptions ought to be informative, enticing and keyword-rich.

Making and selling tools to help with your craft technique

One of the ways I solve the conflict of wanting to make one-off miniatures but needing an income, is by making duplicates of the tools I use to help me with my techniques. So, for example, when I was working in solid polymer clay I designed moulds for my own use and then duplicated them for my customers. You can go so far as to make kits of your favourite techniques. Recently I invented a new stencilling technique for flower making and, of course I was keen to share that as a maker of tool products too, not only because sharing is what I do but because it makes absolute business sense to do so.

Writing and self-publishing

Books can gain you a repetitive monthly 'passive' income which can provide you with a business foundation while you concentrate even more time on your art. If you've ever thought you might teach or write a book, start keeping your ideas right now. Because when you come to get started you'll already have a springboard. No little self-invented hint or trick is too small or too insignificant. Save it all. These days, book sales are a very significant part of our monthly income. In fact, we're planning a follow up to this book to tell you exactly how to start writing your craft teaching books.

Selling Patterns

That sausage dog pattern could be available as a downloadable PDF on Etsy.

You could create SVGs for plotter cutters like Cricut or Silhouette and for laser cutters. Especially if you yourself have used a popular design (of your own) which you are now bored of.

Crowdfunding: Patreon, Ko-Fi, Gofundme, and Kickstarter

Patreon

Patreon is the one that I use most of all and is my favourite. It was absolutely crucial in my 5 year plan. And I credit my patrons for a large part of my current drive and inspiration. Therefore, I give it a lot of weight in this section.

I've found that running a Patreon page helps in several ways. Firstly, it brings your readers and fans into a community, and having a community is a great basis for your business. It helps you focus on your ideal and favourite customers and they are often very honest with you. You can ask for their suggestions, and you can reward their feedback in many different ways. Secondly, of course, they keep another trickle stream of income in. They also act as a focus for your work, reminding you what you need to do next or kicking you into action when you know you haven't shown them something new for a while. If you don't know a lot about Patreon, take a look at what other creators are doing and what they offer in return to their followers, their fans and their customers, in return for a small or larger monthly subscription. There are creators who make almost their entire income out of Patreon, and some of these incomes can be very large indeed. For most of us, the Patreon income is simply a small part of their total. For me it's around a third of my current monthly personal income. Often it tends to be used to reinvest in materials or help from other artists. But there have been months where this income has helped pay an ugly bill.

If you're thinking of starting a Patreon page you need to think where, on the spectrum of accepting help charitably at one end and giving back content or goods at the other, you are going to put yourself. Your first few patrons simply have to love and trust you, because it's a big step for them and there isn't much content to see at first.

Why asking people to be your first patrons is the most difficult thing of all

Getting your first patrons is a big and emotional task but it's one you need to get your head down and do. You really need to aim to keep hustling until you have your first dozen and, somewhat weirdly I would say it's one of the most difficult tasks you may ever undertake, but also one of the most freeing. If you're the kind of person that prides themselves in being pretty self-sufficient and never asking for help. Or if you're the kind of person who refusal often offends, putting your head on the chopping block of possible refusal, especially of a very small amount, seems too dangerous for too small an achievement. Most of us are made that way and to make yourself vulnerable requires a certain amount of humility. This is especially difficult for those of us who have held ourselves together through some of life's emotional and mental knocks.

The reason why we hate "cold calling" our friends and relatives to be our patrons or indeed to help us financially in any way, may be because we fear rejection. In that possible rejection can be the essence of any hang-ups or power struggles inherent in the relationship. It's almost like asking that person if they like or love you. It's excruciatingly humiliating. You may be asking for such a small hand up that refusal can seem petty and absurd and yet some people will refuse, and you know that. However, not asking them (perhaps in case you give them that power and possible pleasure of helping or deciding not to) is also petty and absurd. Yes, you will get refusals and they will be uncomfortable but it can even be a step on your path to acceptance to take that slap and turn the other cheek. Your strength is getting over your fear of asking, and your extra strength is getting over the emotional discomfort of all the feelings that refusal may awaken. Of course, if your friend or relative says yes, that's a glorious affirmation of your friendship and you should be more than grateful. But you should also be grateful to the person who refuses because once you get over that, you are a stronger person by one small step. Allowing yourself to be vulnerable is not only painful at first, it's also extremely freeing and fundamentally strengthening. Go on, test your hang-ups about asking friends for help. If you can get over the possibility of rejection, you're certainly stronger for it. And remember, your first dozen Patrons are your tribe and your superfans and you should be theirs!

"Will Patreon work for me?"

I've seen people complaining about Patreon not working for them. To be honest, I think the people it doesn't seem to work for are the "something for nothing" types, such as those that copy other people's work.

Currently, some people just rake in the YouTube views (and dollars) for re-hashing other artists' ideas. Where they come unstuck on Patreon is they aren't genuinely their ideas. They don't have day-to-day inspiration of their own to share. They have to spend a lot of time making ideas look like their own, and they find it more difficult to be wholly open and genuine one-to-one. And Patreon puts you into a one-to-one situation with every single one of your customers. They are used to YouTube viewers who just come in and don't have to open their wallets. So they're the type of people who are used to getting it for nothing too. Those people maybe don't convert easily to using Patreon. If a creator isn't genuinely interested in their customers and doesn't genuinely appreciate that they have to put real faith in you, well, it shows, and those people won't succeed on Patreon.

So, if you think you can build a Patreon page and suddenly people will just arrive and give you money... They just won't. We all struggle and so we all have a dream that something like that will happen but it doesn't. You have to give value.

Now, what is value for a few dollars on Patreon? Well, in my case it's open sharing of day-to-day ideas. And if you just give one good idea to someone per month that they're going to use in their day to day life, it's going to be more than worth their few dollars. That one thing for them may be a tutorial or it may be some supportive information, or it may just be a hug when they need it if they're a creator too and they're floundering. There are other ways to give back depending on your creative art. If you want to give it a try, just go to Patreon. They will lead you by the hand.

But every patron gained is hard. Like pulling teeth. Especially at the beginning. You know that what you're giving them is worth it. Whether it's the beauty of your work., or in my case the inspiration and support. But you have to get them to "walk through the door", because they can't know that until they do and they're very wary! Micropayments and subscription platforms may be new to them. Especially to my sometimes older demographic. Most people are used to getting your inspiration and support for free. Paying, no matter how little, might be a change for them. This is uncomfortable for both of you until it becomes second nature and just a way of saying thank you for what you give them.

Each patron has different needs. I have one who phones me up for a chat when she needs me. I'm happy to listen. It's reciprocity in action.

All of this can feel very difficult at first, but the more that people come in, the more content you can provide, making it all the more worth it for the patron. Your first patrons are stars, because they genuinely wanted to help you and you have to value them way above the money they help you with. They also give you trust and love, which is priceless. Of course, the main business benefit of Patreon to an artist is that, once you build a following, its money every month. Maybe only a small amount at first. But you can rely on it pretty much every month. So you know you'll be able to put so much time aside every month to do your art, because it's paid.

Look at other people's front pages. Some of which are much better than mine since they've been on it for longer. Have a look at what works. Who's getting the patrons and why? How much does their introductory video inspire you and why?

So, to sum up, Patreon won't work for the "me me me" types. Nor those who really do want to give a good service, but quite honestly can't invest the time upfront. Nor will it work for those who can't bring themselves to ask friends for support which includes money (even if it's only a very small amount). Only for those who naturally and genuinely share and care about their patrons. But you have to swallow your fear of asking and lead your patrons by the hand because they're scared too!

Incidentally, all these platforms are changing as they get tax laws slapped on them and us. Of course, tax has to be paid. I like to think that it takes all the weight of the calculations off your back to know that this is done for you. You can simply write your income down as sales-tax paid in every country of origin. There may well also be an income tax to pay in your own country but you can get an accountant to help you with which box to fill Patreon income in. Some may put it in as royalties or unearned income. Not being an accountant, I'm not sure and will have to refer you back to your own accountant, or the tax authority in your own country.

Ko-fi

Unlike Patreon, Ko-fi is more like a single, one-off thank you platform. Patreon currently doesn't offer a one off payment and relies on the monthly repeatable income which is what it does best - if they diluted it, it may not work. Ko-fi currently puts 100% of contributions into your PayPal account. However, they may fall foul of tax rules over the next few years. Currently, if a friend wants to give me a gift of a coffee, or whatever you want to spend it on, they can and it goes directly into PayPal and that's that. I feel sure this will have to change soon. I have a Ko-fi account and I mention it on my YouTube channel. It's very little used and has been more used by friends to whom I've given useful advice and support. I use it in the same way myself. Because I believe everyone deserves to eat, but I might not want to join everyone else's Patreon or club. I like to use it to say thank you for individual support and advice when it goes above and beyond. It's like a "kindness bank". I like that. As I say, mine isn't currently used much, which might say something about my lack of advertising for this particular platform. I'd like to think Ko-fi has a future, though. It's such a nice idea.

GoFundMe and Kickstarter

If you have a big idea that needs lump sum funding, these platforms are the ones to go for. I can't advise on them, however, as I have no experience. They're certainly worth looking at if your new product idea is really innovative and likely to excite people to want to be part of it, usually in return for some of the first samples of your product when it becomes available.

YouTube

YouTube doesn't pay well unless you're lucky enough to go viral. For example, you might have to get a thousand plays to earn a dollar. That isn't easy if you don't already have a big following, or if you're in a niche market. On the other hand, if you get a hundred thousand plays you could get 100 dollars, and a million might get you a thousand dollars. Most of us will never see that. I have earned a few hundred dollars in the lifetime of our videos. However, if your videos are used to advertise your work anyway, there's not really any loss. The only problem is your poor fans or customers may have to click past an irritating ad first.

Teaching subscriptions and one-to-one mentoring

There are a number of websites for hosting your teaching videos, such as Udemy or Skillshare. You earn a percentage of the total subscriptions based on the popularity of your class.

A fairly new addition at the time of writing is Facebook Appointments, which allows businesses with bookable services to arrange appointments with their customers directly via their Facebook page. This suggests an idea to me: scheduled classes and mentoring. Keep an eye on this

as a potential source of income. I have customers who can't make it to one-to-one classes or who need some personal support. I have never charged for this before, but we really can't afford not to ask for some reciprocal consideration in the form of money. After all, this is a service. It could be good practise to get ready for a more professional approach to a more formal mentoring programme. Mentoring doesn't have to be about wellness, etc. It can cover anyone's subject, including yours.

Affiliate schemes

If you have a popular website, you can join affiliate schemes. This is where you link to products you really like and the seller pays you a very small commission for the sales that are attributable to your link. This is really useful if you are giving people details of where to find craft products for example. You have to state that you have an interest in these recommendations, but you are providing a service to your fans. In our case we probably earn just enough to pay for the time we spend uploading the links, but every little helps, and it doesn't cost your customer any extra. We have an Amazon affiliation and probably earn 100 dollars a year which we spend on craft materials. One of my lovely friends just goes through my links every time she makes a major craft purchase. It works even for other products accessed through my affiliate links. Up to several clicks onward, I believe. If your friends use Amazon a lot this can be a clever little hack while it lasts.

> *Takeaway:* Your business will be more sustainable if you insulate against possible crises by having several income streams. We have three major ones at the moment: the miniatures business, the book business and Patreon. Each brings in some money each month The first is very variable The second is a bit variable within parameters and the last one is fairly fixed. And four minor ones: YouTube, Ko-fi, Amazon Affiliates and Redbubble. It has taken me three years to build some of these. Make a list and work out how you can insulate yourself against the crisis of a slow month on sales of your craft products.

Craft business trends

Craft businesses have trends just the same as the fashion business. Visit craft fairs and trade shows. You aren't going to steal ideas, but rather to have a new tool or technique trigger a development in your own work. For example, the trend in the miniatures world over the last two or three decades has been towards smaller. Initially, it manifested itself as a tendency towards creating room boxes rather than houses. People could afford the time or the money, as well as the space in their houses, for several boxes in place of a house, and makers found them easier to sell. Then, more recently, there was a move towards smaller scales such as 24th, allowing people to fit more in a smaller space. A really new trend in the last few years has been the "book nook", a delightful little room box or scene the size of a large volume or two to sit on a bookshelf. And I'm looking at an idea, not entirely without precedent, along a similar vein to the book nook of just having the front of houses or shops. The contents of the windows and nothing more. Whole street scenes can be created just on one wall of your house. Hanging like a gallery. Almost everyone has space for a street full of houses somewhere in their house. This favours my work, of course, as a producer of individual small items all of which can be displayed across a range of shops.

Keep an eye on trends, but don't always feel compelled to cater your work to them. Sometimes they can spark inspiration, but even if not, it's just good practice to be aware of trends in your particular field.

Have you thought about the wedding business?

There is a definite trend towards more crafty, handmade and vintage-looking weddings. So this is a great place to start looking for opportunities to extend your reach.

Every year millions, if not billions, are spent on weddings and much of that on the little extras like the cards, place mats, cake toppers and bridal favours. Many brides also want to keep replicas of their dress, flowers, cake etc. This business is a dream for the miniaturist and of course, since there are many levels of budget, there is room for many different qualities of work from super expensive top quality work, to little trinkets that the beginner craft business can hone their skills on. Here in Spain, couples give stick pins called "alfileres". Often these are miniature flowers but they can be other symbols and they vary widely in quality from very inexpensive to...well, the sky's the limit for a celebrity wedding!

I recently made the wedding favours, and at the last minute ended up making the cake topper, for my son and his wife's wedding. I stencilled the names of the happy couple and their wedding date onto ribbons and then added stencilled plants on the sides, to form festival style wristbands. At the 11th hour I was also asked to make a cake topper which I really had to rush, and was forced to use some wooden dollies. A little out of my current sphere of experience. My son had done the research and told me that wedding couples will pay handsomely for their own happy couple in their own image! A couple with more money to spend may well give hand crafted items that reflect their personalities and interests to their guests as favours. I was once commissioned to make a number of vegetable crates for the wedding of a greengrocer. I also made 50 sets of miniature false teeth for a dentists wedding. People love the comedy element. Weddings are celebrations and not always straight faced and solemn.

Prepare your offerings and your timescales with plenty of time to spare (double what you think you need). You won't ever be forgiven for getting this wrong. So enter this market knowing that you can't not deliver, as one mistake could cost you any future wedding commissions.

17. Copyright issues

Almost all crafters who have a lovely product will get copied. I don't hold with the "highest compliment" platitude. Most are really just showing their love for your designs. If you teach, as I do, then you should expect copying anyway. However, there are some extremely blatant copying events and I was recently told by a fellow miniaturist that she was offered a thousand pounds if she could teach their makers how I achieved two of my more difficult polymer clay food canes. She says she didn't accept the offer. Hell, I'd have shown them myself for a thousand pounds! That kind of money is hard to earn! I'm not sure the story is entirely true, though I know there's some truth in it. Those items were pretty difficult. Is there anything you can do about this? Not really, no. If that company didn't get a copyist at home, they would get one from East Asia, as there are plenty willing to do it. We simply can't afford to be litigious, and we can't afford to get upset either. It's not fair, but it is going to happen. If that person has gone too far, show them that they are crossing boundaries if necessary, and if the infringement is really serious, you can talk to a solicitor. But be relaxed if the solicitor suggests you let it go and draw a line under it as soon as possible in your own mind.

A 'Trojan horse'

In my business I get regular orders for one each of every craft tool that we sell. Half of these are clearly destined for copyists. But which half? I've started to bury a deliberate "extra" in these goods which is unique to that piece. I can then tell which orders resulted in the latest batch of copies because these companies put their best copyists on the first production and copy with such precision for the first batch that they even copy my deliberate mistakes. Later it's passed down to the minions and the quality drops off. My Trojan horse doesn't help me a whole lot, but it does make it easier to find out who is actually purchasing in order to copy. Sometimes copyists' tricks aren't that clever. A customer used to purchase regularly through family members in case I noticed their serial purchasing. I noticed anyway. They also purchased from a retailer who I sold to wholesale, I noticed this too of course. Research isn't difficult and people who don't tell the truth don't always remember what version of the story they have told to whom. The tricks are many. Unfortunately, the remedies are few.

Incidentally, I don't watermark my photographs. I think it can detract from the image, but it can definitely be useful to watermark images if it doesn't spoil the effect. I have found companies selling cheap copies of my work using my own images. Cheeky!

Don't get jealous, get better.

There will be times along the way when someone will do similar but better, sharper, more attractive work than yours. Especially if you're a teacher. This can be hard to take especially when those people start to get the kudos that you feel you deserve for originating the idea. It's important to ask yourself a few things. Does your envy or annoyance serve any useful purpose? Desiderata states it best: "If you compare yourself with others, you may become vain or bitter, for always there will be greater and lesser persons than yourself".

You have to decide what your boundaries are and make them as relaxed as possible while having a hard edge where you say "this is crossing the boundary". You might have several reasons for getting all rattled because someone has presented work which is beautiful and also similar to yours. Did you teach that technique? In this case, pat yourself on the back for being such a good teacher. People rarely credit the teacher. When they do, it's a joyous thing, but mostly they won't. They enjoy it too when someone tells them they are clever. They are hardly likely to give their moment of joy back to you, even if you really deserve that credit, at least, not very often.

In my opinion, in the world of crafts, you need to develop a healthy attitude to the question of copyright. Otherwise, you could spend the time you might spend creating, simply being a seething mass of resentment, or worse still, lose all your reputation and a fair deal of money in litigation. However, if someone comes back at you on a copyright issue, it's important to have the foundation of knowing when you first did something. Publishing your work on a given date and keeping a record of that date does give you a fair amount of protection. Since people can often learn from a second party or can invent ideas of their own which are identical or very similar to yours, you only need the proof that you did it first to protect yourself from any legal or reputational challenges. If you find that after all someone did something provably first, I think you should graciously hand it to them. Of course sometimes you have to work on your own natural resentment and give yourself a moment to recover from the wound. Then go away and do something amazing spurred on by the desire to show the very best of your own work.

18. The next steps

There come several times in your journey as a craft business when you have to decide whether to take the step to grow...or not. You need to keep revisiting the life balance question. Are you happiest just making or could you cope with staff, outsourcing etc.? Being a Solopreneur, entrepreneur or a hobby crafter are not the same thing at all. This, of course, is beyond the scope of this book but remember this question is coming up. And if you are successful solo, it's going to come up pretty quickly and will require you to be decisive and certain at least about your general direction. Maybe it's time to make a new five year plan. You can revise the plan at any time!

Our very best wishes on your business journey.

Thank you for buying this book - we both hope it helps your business. Good luck with your journey. We would love to hear how you are going, especially if we can help you in any way.

Since you've made it to the very end, we'll ask you if you would please review this book if you can find time. Especially if it has really helped you. This will help our business... and my artist pension plan!

Links

Small Business Networking (support group)
https://www.facebook.com/groups/networking247
I have found this group really informative.

Value added video (and Pinterest video marketing)
https://valueadded.video/work-with-me/

Brand Story Project (Branding)
https://snowballcommunications.co.uk/index.php/brand-story-hub/

.

About the authors

Angie Scarr

Before spending the last 30 years running her own miniatures business for which she is internationally known, Angie Scarr spent 5 years making non-competitive play equipment. This makes 35 of her 37 working years self-employed in the craft world. Angie is the author of two best selling dolls house miniature craft books and 9 more, successful, self-published titles and translated editions. Plus a biography, Making It Small and a non-fiction lifestyle book under the pseudonym Littleoldladywho. She has also written a business column and projects for Dolls House And Miniature Scene Magazine. Latterly her husband Frank has taken the reins of the miniatures business, leaving Angie to concentrate on inventing and teaching new crafts techniques, and her other love: inspiring other creatives by writing and sharing ideas.

Kira Swales

With a degree in creative writing, Kira Swales has a strong background in the craft and textiles industry, along with over six year's experience in ecommerce and copywriting. Kira lives in Manchester with her partner James, one really friendly cat, and one really grumpy cat. When she's not working on SEO, she's normally either behind her sewing machine or at the post office, running her own part-time creative business.

Thanks and acknowledgements

Angie

I know it may seem to be a bit weird to thank your coauthor, but I really do want to thank Kira for coming on board with this project. To me, the opportunity to work with my talented daughter has been such a joy especially because it means that she's not only adding her skill and knowledge but she's also wrangling mine into some sort of shape. The "frustration" hair-pulling cartoon is also by Kira. I know she felt like that a few times during this project.

As always, I want to thank my Patrons. If you have read this far, you will know that Patreon can be an important cornerstone in the support for innovation in the creative arts. So, I also want to thank Patreon, the company, and Jack, its CEO. I am one of many thousands of creatives who are benefitting from his simple but hugely important idea. That artists don't have to starve when there is a world of people who can benefit from their work and can support them according to their means.

So, special thanks to all of my patrons for your support, not only financial, but practical and, in many cases, advisory. I'm indebted to Angie Grace Coloring Books for her insights into the craft business in the United States, and to Karen Isaacson and Rene Rushing.

To all my Patrons: Riemkje Boom, Deborah Koepp, Madeleine Mac Donald, Michele, Countess Viviana, Alexander Baytchev, Brezavaqt, Shelley Wylie, Mary Myers, Denise Pinnell, Spellbound Miniatures, Ruth Moe, Rothes, Carol Medina, Roberta Solari, Dr. Deborah Lee, Gosia Suchodolska, Christine M McKechnie, Karen S Sullivan, Gabriel Kramer, Petra Suijker, Gail Barlow, Kimberly Gates, Suzie Aguilar, Kerstin Fischer, David Assenti, Karen Kneezle, Kimberly Gregory, Sarah Skala , Jennifer Gilmour, Susan, Pam Blume, Carla Speed McNeil, Karen Isaacson, J P Hall, Sebastian Fulmer, Charity , Martin Andres, Linda Nielsen, Julia Hood, Ann Storey, M Carmen García Morín, Erin Kogan-Garrett, Karen Rollinson, Matilde Mora Rodríguez, Cheryl La Greca Markov, Gill Bayes, Maryse Cuypers, Toni Ballinger, Barbara, Anke Humpert, Kerstin Wildrose, Anne Erlandson-Foss, Marta Teran Rodriguez, Macie Kaye, Gillian Thompson, Tee Bylo, Barbara Taylor-Harris, Dominique Ceuppers, Sandi Smith, Tina Knuth, Kasia Win, Karin Kathrina Sørensen, Hellie Durans, Robyn Donald, Tara Jane Susie Langworthy, Janette Murphy, Loredana Tonetti, Essie Kenneway, Lesley, Sean Sullivan, Michaela Stange, Jeannette Fishwick, Rachel Taylor, Nicola Croad, Roslyn Hill, Rosemary Mulley, Helen Cruickshank, Lucy Rider, Grethe Holme Jantzen, Stephanie Ryan, Natalie Martin-Burrows.

Also to Ann Bromley for information used in this book; Emily Dewsnap, for research; and the people of my pueblo who constantly support me including, but not exclusively, Maria Luisa (Mama), Mari Lou, Angeles, Hermenegildo (El Mere) and Eduardo (El Pimo). For ideas and inspiration about business marketing, thanks to Jennifer Gilmour, Kate Tyson of the Brand Story Project, Naomi Jane Johnson of Value Added Video and Pinterest Video Marketing, and Alan Iumb for valuable advice about 'utility' in the pricing section.

Kira

Firstly, I want to thank my mum for encouraging me to collaborate with her on this project, for being patient with me when I've felt overwhelmed, and for passing on the gift (and occasional curse) of creativity. I also want to thank my partner James for always supporting me on my journey. Finally, thanks to every customer who takes the time to give small businesses their 5 star reviews, it really makes a big difference to all of us.

We would both like to thank Frank for layout and publishing work and steering us in the right direction many times over the years in both of our craft business enterprises, for never complaining about money spent on crafting, and for generally having our backs.

Here are the ways you can connect with us, and get to hear about any future publications:

Like, share and follow our pages

Please join my Patrons on Patreon:
www.patreon.com/angie_scarr

If I have helped you with advice etc. please feel free to buy me a coffee **ko-fi.com/angiescarr**

Angie's social media pages:
www.facebook.com/angiescarr.miniatures
www.facebook.com/Littleoldladywho
www.facebook.com/groups/yourcreativebusiness *(Your creative business)*

Join Self publishing and Author group arts and crafts tutorials FB page if you are interested in writing a how-to book on your craft.
www.facebook.com/groups/selfpubauthors/

www.linkedin.com/in/kira-swales

Further reading:
Coming Soon. Your Craft Business - Workbook: Practical, achievable business development steps in a simple informal journal style.

Watch out for an upcoming title on self-publishing your own craft books and tutorials.

Join our mailing list for more information at
www.angiescarr.co.uk/UK_index.html#frontpage_contact

Visit my website and buy my miniatures books for all your craft minded friends.
www.angiescarr.com

Printed in Great Britain
by Amazon